LORD PENGO

LORD
PENGO

A Comedy in Three Acts
by S. N. BEHRMAN
Suggested by his New Yorker *series,*
"The Days of Duveen"

RANDOM HOUSE · NEW YORK

for

CHARLES BOYER, AGNES MOOREHEAD, BRIAN BEDFORD,
RUTH WHITE, HENRY DANIELL, EDMON RYAN,
CLIFF HALL, BETTY SINCLAIR, LEE RICHARDSON,
LAURIE MAIN, REYNOLDS EVANS.

LORD PENGO *was first presented by Paul Gregory and Amy Lynn at the Royale Theatre, New York City, on November 19, 1962, with the following cast:*

(IN ORDER OF APPEARANCE)

FILBERT	Laurie Main
DEREK PENGO	Brian Bedford
LORD PENGO	Charles Boyer
JOHNSON	Reynolds Evans
PRIMROSE DRURY	Ruth White
WALTER CANNON BRINK III	Edmon Ryan
LADY WINFIELD	Betty Sinclair
WILFRED OLIVER	Lee Richardson
ENOCH DRURY	Henry Daniell
MISS SWANSON	Agnes Moorehead
SYLVESTER SCHMITT	Cliff Hall
VICKERS	*This character did not appear in the Broadway production.*

Directed by Vincent J. Donehue
Settings by Oliver Smith
Lighting by Jean Rosenthal
Costumes by Lucinda Ballard

SYNOPSIS OF SCENES

ACT ONE

Lord Pengo's Gallery, Grafton Street, London. May, 1933.

ACT TWO

Lord Pengo's Gallery, Fifth Avenue, New York. October 1933.

SCENE 1: Midafternoon.
SCENE 2: Late afternoon, the same day.
SCENE 3: Early evening, the same day.

ACT THREE

Lord Pengo's Gallery, Fifth Avenue, New York. Five years later.

GUIDE TO THE WORKS OF ART
VISIBLE AT LORD PENGO'S

The Adoration of the Shepherds—Giorgione (1473–1510) A celebrated painting now hanging simultaneously in the National Gallery in Washington and at Lord Pengo's. There was a great flurry over the attribution of this picture, since the foremost authority in the world on Renaissance art, Bernard Berenson, vacillated between assigning it to Giorgione and Titian. This brings me to another work of art referred to, though not visible in this play, Bernard Berenson. He lived in royal style just outside Florence, Italy, and died several years ago, at the age of ninety-two. I knew him. He was a man of fascinating complexity and a great talker. The fracas over this picture caused a break between him and Lord Pengo's predecessor, Lord Duveen of Millbank. Lord Duveen paid Berenson handsomely for his advice. Berenson's final decision that The Adoration of the Shepherds was by Titian resulted in a permanent rift between him and Lord Duveen. It also considerably disturbed Lord Pengo.

Head of a Little Girl—Settignano (1428–1464) Settignano's exquisite head of a little boy is a showpiece in the National Gallery. Possibly he preferred little boys, but it suited me to have him do a little girl. Who knows that, in a tolerant moment, he didn't?

The Circumcision—Masaccio (1401–1428) Masaccio occupies a conspicuous place in the history of Italian painting. There is no record of his ever having done a Circumcision. There also is no record of his not having done one. As it suited me to improvise a little girl for Settignano, it also suited me to permit Masaccio to divert himself by painting a Circumcision. This is one of the advantages of fiction over history. The former is more relaxed.

Mrs. Siddons as the Tragic Muse—Sir Joshua Reynolds (1723-1792) Of this picture Sir Thomas Lawrence said that it was the "finest portrait ever painted under the canopy of heaven." That is a large statement, and considering that it was made by a rival artist, extremely generous.

Portrait of Queen Henrietta Maria with the Dwarf Jeffrey Hudson and the Monkey—Sir Anthony Van Dyck— (1599-1641) This famous painting is now hanging in the National Gallery in Washington on loan from Lord Pengo.

Aristotle Contemplating the Bust of Homer—Rembrandt (1606-1669) This painting was held at various times by Lord Duveen. In the play it belongs to Lord Pengo. Though there are great similarities between the two men, there are also salient differences. Were it not for these differences, I don't think I could have written this play.

S. N. BEHRMAN

ACT ONE

ACT ONE

Scene: LORD PENGO'S *office—London, May, 1933. A high-ceilinged room done in the style of the Brothers Adam. The furnishings and decorations are a collection of authentic antiques and paintings—mostly of the Italian schools. The woodwork is painted a soft white and the walls are finished in a striped paper overlayed with a meandering morning-glory motif in several shades of blue-gray. Center stage on an oval carpet is* PENGO'S *desk and chair. In front of the desk is a small period stool. To the right of the desk is a small open armchair. At left is a door to the outer office and down from this door is an occasional chair. Leaning against the wall are two framed paintings with inventory tags attached. At the center of the back wall is a large window looking out onto the London street. To the left of this is a pedestal with a piece of sculpture on it. To the right is a wall table with a vase of flowers, over which hangs Masaccio's* The Circumcision. *In the corner of the right wall is a concealed door to an inner hall. Downstage right is an easel with the Allendale Giorgione on it. There is a traveler rod and drapery over the painting, so that it may be covered. There are several other paintings on the walls and a chandelier hangs from the ceiling.*

At rise: FILBERT, LORD PENGO'S *factotum, is fussing with the Allendale which he has just brought in.* FILBERT *is very Cockney. He has been a steward on an English ship on which* PENGO *has made innumerable crossings. Lik-*

3

ing his service, PENGO *asked him one day whether he would care to leave the sea to become his valet.* FILBERT *left the sea. Latterly* PENGO *has permitted* FILBERT *to valet the pictures also. While* FILBERT *is making adjustments to the easel of the Allendale,* DEREK PENGO, LORD PENGO'S *son, comes in. He is a charming, sensitive, diffident young Englishman of twenty-four.*

DEREK   Ah, Filbert. What's the Giorgione doing in here?

FILBERT   Your father ordered me to 'ave it placed in 'ere, Mr. Derek, as 'e is expectin' Mr. Drury to come to 'ave a look at it.

DEREK   Oh, Drury's coming, is he?

FILBERT   Yes, Mr. Derek. 'E 'as an appointment. May I ask what this is, Mr. Derek?

DEREK   It is a very famous picture, Filbert. The Adoration of the Shepherds. Do you like it?

FILBERT *(With a casual glance at the picture)*   Oh, it's fetchin', Mr. Derek. No doubt about that.

DEREK   Well, Filbert, how do you like the new life my father has provided for you?

FILBERT   When I was steward on the *Berengaria* I weyted on your father many crossings. 'E's a very kind and amiable gentleman, your father, except when 'e's angry.

DEREK *(Smiles at him sympathetically)*   The exceptions are frequent, I'm afraid!

FILBERT   I'd be quite 'appy 'ere if it wasn't for these Eyetalian pictures. I 'ave difficulty masterin' their names.

4

They're bitter, those names and when I mess 'em up your father boils over a bit . . . This one 'ere for instance— (*He mops his perspiring brow*) 'E's a tough one for sure. Jar— Jar—

DEREK Giorgione.

FILBERT I 'ave tried. I 'ave studied. But it just won't roll off my tongue, Mr. Derek.

DEREK Don't worry, Filbert. My father sometimes forgets the names of the artists himself. To him they're all Pengos.

FILBERT Your father 'its the ceilin' every time I . . . I sometimes wish, Mr. Derek . . .

DEREK Yes, Filbert?

FILBERT (*Pleading desperately for a reasonable accommodation*) That your father would cheynge their names —couldn't 'e just give 'em some good English names?

DEREK (*Delighted with this*) I'll suggest it to him, Filbert!

(LORD PENGO *enters. He is a handsome, beautifully-dressed Englishman of Hungarian extraction, in the prime of life. He radiates energy and good will; he gives the impression of a man who wants everybody around him to have as good a time as possible. He really takes an enormous interest in people and feels warmth toward them, except when crossed; when that happens, his temper is uncontrollable and apoplectic; he has, in fact, the high coloring of the apoplectic. He enjoys his own career, is conscious of giving a "good performance," and would*

5

like it if other people got fun out of it, as he does himself. He has an infectious laugh which rings out whenever he is amused—not only by the foibles of others, but by his own)

DEREK   I've just got a wonderful idea from Filbert, Father!

PENGO   That's no surprise to me. Filbert is always very stimulating. (*To* FILBERT)   Thank you, Filbert.

FILBERT   Thank you, my Lord.
    (FILBERT *goes out.* DEREK *is smiling*)

PENGO   What are you laughing at?

DEREK   Filbert. He's marvelous.

PENGO   Sometimes I think I made a mistake when I took him off the sea. He was such a good steward.

DEREK   So Drury's finally coming, is he?

PENGO   Yes. Took a lot of doing. He's got it into his stubborn head that this Giorgione's a Titian.

DEREK   What else is on the program for today?

PENGO   Walter Cannon Brink. The railroad king from San Francisco.

DEREK   What's he after?

PENGO   He wants an English eighteenth-century portrait for his private Pullman car.

DEREK   Why can't he look at the scenery?

PENGO   Because it doesn't cost anything!

DEREK   Is Primrose coming with Brink?

PENGO   Naturally—she wants to look at the chinoiserie.

DEREK   (*Teasing him*)   We won't deny her that opportunity, will we, Father?

PENGO   (*Teasing back*)   Of course not. I love Prim and
haven't the heart to deny her anything! By the way,
Derek, I've almost persuaded Prim to build a house in
New York.

DEREK   If you've almost persuaded her she's persuaded.

PENGO   (*Enjoying laying out his strategy to* DEREK)   As
Walter Cannon Brink is crazy about her, I am going to
suggest to him that he wants a house in New York too.

DEREK   Packed to the roof with the best Pengos.

PENGO   What else?

DEREK   Really, Father! The way you mix up love with
architecture!

PENGO   They harmonize, my boy . . . Also, Derek, a
detail . . .

DEREK   Ah! A detail!

PENGO   I have placed the Red Boy of Goya in the passage
on the way to the Chinese Gallery. So be sure you take
Prim through that way. I have a strong feeling—that
Prim may want to *adopt* the Red Boy.

DEREK   Busy afternoon! Crowded with detail!

PENGO   (*Turns to the Allendale*)   It's all nothing, Derek

7

—small change—compared to Drury and the Allendale. He's the toughest of my customers—I can't get close to him.

DEREK   Who can? He walked out on Prim. And Daphne, his own daughter, is afraid of him, can't talk to him.

PENGO   He has a peculiar effect on me—makes me nervous —very nervous. (*Goes to the Allendale, contemplates it gloomily*)   It's going to be a tussle—a tremendous tussle —to sell him this Giorgione.

DEREK   Isn't Berenson a little doubtful that it is a Giorgione?

PENGO   (*Sharply*)   Thirty years ago he said it *was!*

DEREK   That's a long time ago.

PENGO   I think I can persuade Berenson to recover his original impulse. Now, Derek, help me to anticipate Drury's objections, will you? Let's—practice! *Be* Drury for a few minutes.

DEREK   Now, Dad! If I could be Drury—with that vast fortune and that arctic exposure—do you think I'd be working for an impulsive Hungarian like you?

PENGO   (*Severely*)   Don't joke, Derek. This is serious. Help me.

DEREK   All right. I'll try.

PENGO   (*Going into his act*)   Sit down, Mr. Drury, so I can show it to you properly.

8

DEREK (*He has seen* DRURY. *He now imitates that glacial, Olympian manner*) Thank you.

PENGO Now then— (*He takes his stance before the Allendale*) It is a question of this magnificent, unparalleled Giorgione. I own the greatest pictures in the world, Mr. Drury. This is the greatest picture I have ever owned. The fact is, Mr. Drury, I have been for three days—since this greatest of all masterpieces came into my possession—in a state bordering on exaltation. Haven't been able to eat or sleep . . . (*Stops, annoyed with* DEREK) Well! Why don't you say something?

DEREK Because Drury never does. He knows that silence makes people uncomfortable.

PENGO (*Almost shouts*) Don't overdo it! Drury does speak sometimes. He often says no.

DEREK Now, Father, don't lose your temper with me. You might do it with Drury and that would be fatal. Try again.

PENGO (*Swallows his pride, gets control of himself and goes again into his spiel*) Look at it, Mr. Drury—feast your eyes upon it—the Allendale Giorgione. It is not a painting merely. It is music. Colored music.

DEREK That's pretty.

PENGO Shut up! You know that Giorgione died when he was thirty-two years old. There are not in the world ten pictures that are indisputably his own. This is one of them.

DEREK (*Imitates* DRURY'*s astringent tone*) When you say

9

"indisputably," you exaggerate. There is considerable dispute. No one in the world knows more about Italian pictures than Bernard Berenson. And Berenson says it is not a Giorgione but a Titian.

PENGO   Yes, but before that—thirty years ago—Berenson pronounced it a Giorgione.

DEREK   I prefer his mature opinion to his juvenile one.

PENGO   I assure you, my dear Mr. Drury, that Berenson will pronounce it a Giorgione.

DEREK   Do you add prophecy to your other accomplishments, Lord Pengo?

PENGO   (*Loses his temper, blurts out*)   Drury would never say that!

DEREK   (*Defending his interpretation*)   How do you know he wouldn't?

PENGO   (*Who knows that that is just what* DRURY *would say*)   I just know!

DEREK   Sorry. I'm only improvising.

PENGO   Try again. (*Gets a grip on himself and returns to the attack*)   I assure you, my dear Mr. Drury, that Berenson will pronounce it a Giorgione.

DEREK   I shall wait for Berenson to change his mind. (*Turns to go*)   Good morning, Lord Pengo.

PENGO   (*Mutters*)   That's better!

DEREK   (*Stops*)   Assuming, Lord Pengo . . .

PENGO Yes, Mr. Drury?

DEREK . . . that this picture *is* by Giorgione—

PENGO Yes, Mr. Drury?

DEREK What will you ask for it?

PENGO That's a good question. This picture is unique. There is no other like it in the world. It is priceless. (*Smiles at* DEREK) You are businessman enough to know, my dear Mr. Drury, that no matter what you pay for the priceless, you are getting it cheap!

DEREK (*His lips have silently mouthed his father's words —he has heard them so often*) Well, there you are! I've given you a chance to use your favorite slogan.

PENGO It is not a slogan, Derek, it is a sound principle. It appeals to bargain-hunters.

DEREK (*Laughs*) You *are* wonderful, Father. So—resilient!

PENGO Well, what do you think, Derek? Will Drury see the light?

DEREK (*More soberly*) Don't ask me what *I* think, Dad.

PENGO (*Sharply*) Why not?

DEREK Because, one: my opinion is unimportant. Two: it might make you angry.

PENGO And three: I wouldn't act on it! No doubt about it, when your mother bore you, she gave birth to a conscience.

(JOHNSON *comes in. He is tall, bald, superb—an emperor in a frock coat and striped trousers*)

JOHNSON Mrs. Drury, Mr. Walter Cannon Brink. Lady Winfield is waiting. She says she has an appointment.

PENGO Show Mrs. Drury and Mr. Brink in.

JOHNSON Yes, my Lord.
(JOHNSON *goes*)

PENGO Derek, go to the reception room, will you, and chat with Lady Winfield for a bit?

DEREK Fine.

PENGO She's a dear woman, unfortunately down on her luck, but I think I can do something for her.

DEREK Well, if you think you can do something for her —she'll soon be swimming in affluence!
(*He goes*)

JOHNSON (*Returns*) Mrs. Enoch Drury and Mr. Walter Cannon Brink.
(JOHNSON *goes out.* MRS. ENOCH DRURY *and* MR. WALTER CANNON BRINK, III, *enter.* PRIMROSE DRURY, *between forty-five and fifty, was, in her girlhood, a stage beauty and is still lovely; she is one of those women whose charm is perennial; she will be enchanting when she is seventy. Incapable of affectation herself, she penetrates pretension in others through her natural acute sense of observation. At the same time she is incorrigibly romantic and wants to be loved and to be herself in love.* WALTER CANNON BRINK, III, *is a multimillionaire*

*who has pulled himself up by virtue of an acci-
dental association with men harder and more ruth-
less than himself—like* ENOCH DRURY, *for example,
whose partner he once was. The gnawing envy
and hatred of his life is* DRURY, *to whom he owes
his eminence and who has made him aware of the
debt. Outwardly,* BRINK *is a mild, timid little man
of fifty, with the appearance of a store clerk who
will never get a raise. When his visitors come in,
they find* PENGO *in rapt contemplation of the Giorgione. He gives the effect of being jolted out of a
trance. He wheels to greet them)*

PENGO My dear Primrose!

PRIMROSE Hello, Joe, how's every little thing?

PENGO Wally! How are you?

BRINK Greetings!

PENGO Delighted to see you . . . Well, Wally! Enjoying
yourself?

BRINK That's just what I'm not. Can't wait to get on
that boat and back to San Francisco!

PENGO And with your darling Prim here! Come now,
Wally! That's not very gallant!

PRIMROSE With me, Wally's on one subject all the time.
Marriage. He's got no what-you-might-call general con-
versation.

BRINK I don't know how many times I've proposed to
Prim, Joe.

PRIMROSE   At lunch today was number eight.

PENGO   She keeps count, Wally. That should encourage you.

PRIMROSE   No such thing. I've got other ideas and Wally knows it.

BRINK   Did you ever hear the like, Joe, Prim being faithful to a man who's deserted her? What do you make of that?

PRIMROSE   I'm eccentric, Wally. Better make up your mind to that. (*Looking at the Allendale*)   What's this, Joe?

PENGO (*He has been waiting for this*)   The Allendale Giorgione. Greatest picture I ever owned!

PRIMROSE   What are they all doing?

PENGO   It is called The Adoration of the Shepherds.

PRIMROSE   Where are the sheep?

PENGO   In another picture. Do you like sheep?

PRIMROSE   I love sheep.

PENGO   I'll show you a picture with sheep.

BRINK   Don't care for pictures of babies!

PENGO   Oh, but, my dear Wally, *this* baby!

BRINK   How much?

PENGO (*Has been waiting for this also*)   Not for sale!

BRINK (*The picture becomes instantly desirable; piqued and irritated*)   Why not?

PENGO (*As if eager to drop the subject*) Earmarked for another client.

BRINK (*Snarls*) I can guess who!

PENGO (*Pleasantly*) Can you?

BRINK (*Hating every syllable of the name*) Enoch Drury.

PENGO Now, Wally, don't pry—trade secret.

BRINK *He* gets everything.

PRIMROSE Everything but what makes him happy.

BRINK (*Jealous*) He got you!

PRIMROSE He got me all right, but he didn't want to keep me.

BRINK (*To* PRIMROSE) And you're still hankering. You're only here now because you know Drury's coming.

PENGO How do you know that, Wally?

BRINK Because she told me and you told her!

PENGO I told you that in confidence, Prim.

PRIMROSE Sorry, Joe.

BRINK (*This is a sore point with him; to* PENGO) Drury's Number One with you, Joe. Everybody knows that.

PENGO (*Alleviating his pain*) Come, come, Wally—I haven't done badly by you, have I? You have a beautiful collection. I showed you the Van Dyck in the National Gallery the other day, didn't I? Now, the one I sold you is better. Didn't you see that it was better?

BRINK   I wouldn't give up mine for half a dozen of the National Gallery's.

PENGO *(Beams at him)*   Well! There you are!
(DEREK *comes back*)

PRIMROSE   Derek!

DEREK   Prim!

PENGO   You know my son and heir, Derek Pengo. Mr. Walter Cannon Brink.
(BRINK *and* DEREK *shake hands*)

DEREK   Excuse me, Dad. Lady Winfield says she has to make an early train back to the country.

PENGO   I'll see her in a minute. *(To* BRINK*)*   Must see Lady Winfield on your account, Wally.

BRINK   On my account!

PENGO   She owns an absolutely marvelous portrait of her great-great-great-grandmother by Hoppner which I mean to pry out of her for you.

BRINK   What are you going to soak me for her?

PENGO   Depends on Lady Winfield. She may turn out to be a sharp bargainer. But I think I can get it for you for a mere forty thousand.

BRINK   Dollars or pounds?

PENGO Wally, be serious. Pounds.

BRINK That's a hell of a lot to pay for a great-grand-mother.

PENGO Ah! But in the portrait *this* great-grandmother is twenty years old and ravishingly beautiful.

PRIMROSE Where's the chin-wah-soree you were telling me about, Joe?

PENGO Derek, show Primrose the chinoiserie.

PRIMROSE Want *you* to show it to me, Joe. I won't be-lieve it's the real McCoy till *you* show it to me!

PENGO Well, *look* at it with Derek and then I'll *show* it to you.

DEREK You look at it with me, Prim, it won't cost you anything.

PRIMROSE I love looking at things with you, Derek, I don't have to decide anything. (*To* BRINK) Don't you want to see it, Wally?

BRINK Want to talk to Joe a minute.

PENGO Certainly. (*To* DEREK) Provide some tea.

PRIMROSE Tea! I've been drowning in tea since I got to London. Haven't you got some good hot Java?

PENGO Derek, coffee.

DEREK Certainly.
(PRIMROSE *and* DEREK *go out*)

BRINK Nice boy you got.

PENGO Best in the world. Gets out of hand here and there . . .

BRINK Same with my boy. Great disappointment. Drinks and wenches.

PENGO Oh, nothing like that with Derek.

BRINK Prim tells me he's got a crush on her daughter, Daphne.

PENGO Absolutely smitten.

BRINK Daphne takes after her father. Tough baby.

PENGO Prefer that to a soft baby. That's my worry about Derek—soft baby.

BRINK (*Lovelorn*) Awful sunk, Joe.

PENGO Why?

BRINK Prim.

PENGO Plenty of fish in the sea, Wally, for a man of your resources.

BRINK Prim is the fish I want.

PENGO Will you take my advice, Wally?

BRINK You're the only one I can talk to, Joe.

PENGO (*His line of action taut*) How would you like to spend the weekend with me at Winthrop Castle? Lord Shillinghurst's. One of England's most beautiful homes.

BRINK But Prim is sailing!

18

PENGO (*Airily*) Let her sail.

BRINK I'm lonely in Europe. Awful lonely.

PENGO But London is a marvelous city—so much to do here.

BRINK Maybe for you—not for me. I'm going to tell you something, Joe. One night—couple of weeks ago—I got so blue and lonely I asked the manicure girl in the hotel what to do, where to go.

PENGO Did she tell you?

BRINK She told me.

PENGO Did you take her?

BRINK I took her.

PENGO Did you enjoy it?

BRINK I didn't. She didn't.

PENGO Too bad.

BRINK It's a matter of pride with me, Joe.

PENGO What is?

BRINK Not to get things—you know what I mean, Joe—for money.

PENGO Want to be loved for yourself alone. That it?

BRINK (*Happy to be understood*) That's it! That's why—when I take out a girl like that—I don't let 'em know I'm a rich man. I act stingy.

PENGO   I'm sure that you are very convincing.

BRINK   You see, Joe . . . Ever since I was knee-high to a grasshopper I've been in love with Prim. Ever tell you how I met her?

PENGO   Don't believe you did.

BRINK   She was one of the Three Dandies.

PENGO   *Was she?* Who were they?

BRINK   Father and daughter act. Two sisters and their father. They danced. Saw them with Enoch Drury when they played Sacramento.

PENGO   And you both fell in love with Primrose?

BRINK   Enoch got her. I was stuck with the other two Dandies.

PENGO   Oh, yes. I'd heard you and Drury married sisters.

BRINK   I didn't like the sister much but I married her anyway. Because Prim wanted me to. After she died and Prim and Drury got separated, I thought sure Prim would marry me. But she won't.

PENGO   Be guided by me, old boy. Let Primrose sail by herself and come with me to Winthrop Castle. I'll see that Lady Shillinghurst invites some attractive women down.

BRINK   (*In a panic*)   Don't do that, Joe. Please!

PENGO   Why not?

BRINK   I know those kind of women. They scare me. Any

20

minute they're liable to break into French. I don't even understand their English.

PENGO   All right. Nobody there but you and me. In two weeks we'll sail to New York together.

BRINK   That'll be wonderful, Joe. Gosh, you're a real friend.

PENGO   (*Demonstrating his friendship*)   Why don't you leave San Francisco, Wally? Why don't you build a house in New York?

BRINK   I like San Francisco. New York scares me almost as much as Europe does.

PENGO   (*Casually*)   Prim's building a house in New York.

BRINK   (*Surprised*)   Is she? She didn't tell *me!*

PENGO   (*With an engaging smile at him*)   I told *her!* She's tired of living in that gloomy hotel Drury gave her when he separated from her.
      (JOHNSON *comes in*)

JOHNSON   Mr. Wilfred Oliver, and Lady Winfield is still waiting.

PENGO   Quite. Show Lady Winfield up. Ask Mr. Oliver to wait. Take Mr. Brink to the Chinese Gallery. And, Johnson, get me Sir William Fitzpatrick on the phone. Urgent. (JOHNSON *goes out as* PENGO *walks* BRINK *to the door*)   It's settled then. You're not sailing with Primrose. You're waiting for me.

BRINK   Can I count on you, Joe?

21

PENGO Absolutely.

BRINK (*With an excess of pride*) I'll tell Prim. Maybe you're right. She's been counting on me too much. I've been too steady.

PENGO That's the spirit, Wally.
  (BRINK *goes out. The telephone rings*)

PENGO (*On the phone*) Ah, Sir William! How are you? . . . Never better . . . I'm calling you about a New York job . . . Very interesting—a house on Fifth Avenue for one of my American clients. Walter C. Brink the Third . . . What about lunch on Friday, to meet Mr. Brink? . . . Fine . . . Think this will interest you very much, Sir William.
  (*He hangs up.* JOHNSON *shows in* LADY WINFIELD. *She is a fragile, shy, gray-haired British aristocrat, rather shabbily dressed.* PENGO'S *manner to her is exquisitely courteous*)

JOHNSON Lady Winfield . . .
  (JOHNSON *disappears*)

PENGO My dear Lady Winfield, it is very good of you to come.

LADY WINFIELD Thank you, Lord Pengo.

PENGO Please sit down . . . May I say, Lady Winfield, without beating about the bush, that I am madly in love with your great-great-great-grandmother!

LADY WINFIELD Very nice of you to say so, Lord Pengo.

PENGO Hoppner never did anything better.

22

LADY WINFIELD   We hate to part from her.

PENGO (*Gently*)   What do you want for your Hoppner, Lady Winfield?

LADY WINFIELD   Well, I thought . . . my husband thought . . . as you know, my husband has been invalided for a long time . . . otherwise . . .

PENGO   My understanding was that you would discuss it fully with your husband, arrive at a price, and tell me what it is.

LADY WINFIELD   Yes, Lord Pengo.

PENGO (*Patiently*)   Have you arrived at a figure?

LADY WINFIELD   Yes, we have. As you yourself admit, Lord Pengo, it is a very fine Hoppner . . . (*She simply cannot bring herself to name the sum, which now seems staggering to her*)   We thought therefore . . .

PENGO   The figure, Lady Winfield?

LADY WINFIELD (*Shuts her eyes, holds on to the arms of the chair, leaps into the abyss*)   Eighteen thousand pounds. (*There is a silence.* LADY WINFIELD *opens her eyes. She sees that* PENGO *is staring at her, shocked. In agony, she starts to apologize*)   You see . . . we are in a most . . . it is humiliating to . . . but no one else has seen the picture . . . with a view to, that is . . . you expressed such enthusiasm for it . . . my husband thought . . .

PENGO   Forgive me if I tell you, Lady Winfield, that I am quite shocked.

LADY WINFIELD (*Starts to get up*) In that case, if you came to see us again . . . and talked to my husband . . .

PENGO (*Keeps her from getting up*) No, no, Lady Winfield . . . please . . .

LADY WINFIELD My husband gets tired so easily. I wished to spare him.

PENGO Another interview will not be necessary. I have said that I am shocked, and I am. That you should consent to part with such an exquisite work of art . . . (*His voice quivers at the betrayal*) for the paltry sum of eighteen thousand pounds!
(*He turns away to master his indignation*)

LADY WINFIELD (*Quite at sea*) I am afraid—that I don't . . .

PENGO The very least—the rock-bottom least—that you should sell a Hoppner of this quality for is twenty-five thousand pounds. I should be honored, I should be grateful, if you would let me have your great-great-great-grandmother for twenty-five thousand pounds.

LADY WINFIELD Lord Pengo . . . I . . .

PENGO Is it—as we say in America—a deal?

LADY WINFIELD (*On the verge of tears*) You are very kind.

PENGO Oh, my dear Lady Winfield, it is not my kindness, it's my customer's; and I assure you, he can well afford to give you your profit—and mine as well. (*At his telephone*) Vickers, I have concluded the arrangement for Lady Winfield's Hoppner. Twenty-five thousand pounds. Make out the check. (*He buzzes for* JOHNSON, *who appears directly*) Are you returning to the country, Lady Winfield?

LADY WINFIELD   Yes, I only came in to . . .

PENGO   My car will take you to Waterloo. (*To* JOHNSON) Tell Crutch. Look up the train. I shall want Crutch here. The House of Lords at three-thirty.

JOHNSON   Yes, my Lord.
(*He exits*)

PENGO (*Walking* LADY WINFIELD *to the door*) My comptroller will give you your check, Lady Winfield.

LADY WINFIELD (*Hesitates*) You have been so very kind, Lord Pengo . . . more than generous . . .

PENGO   Something on your mind, your Ladyship?

LADY WINFIELD   You were good enough to say . . . that you would provide a good home. Would it be presumptuous to ask . . .

PENGO   Where she will live? Not at all. For the time being, in Mr. Walter C. Brink's private Pullman car.

LADY WINFIELD (*Utterly bewildered*) I'm afraid I don't understand . . .

PENGO   Mr. Brink is president of a great railroad. He shuttles between New York, Palm Beach and Seattle in his private car. Your great-great-great-grandmother will see America as no Englishwoman has ever seen it before.

LADY WINFIELD She'll be so restless!

PENGO No, she won't. She'll spend most of her time in San Francisco.

LADY WINFIELD San Francisco! That's so very far away.

PENGO I think I can promise you that your great-great-great-grandmother will soon be moving to New York.

LADY WINFIELD New York. Oh, that will bring her so much closer, won't it?

PENGO When your husband is better, you might pop over to see her as my guests.

LADY WINFIELD I don't know how to thank you, Lord Pengo.

PENGO Delighted, Lady Winfield. Delighted. Good luck . . . (*She goes.* PENGO *goes to the phone*) Put in a call to my office in New York. I want to talk to Miss Swanson. Make it for five o'clock. I'll be back from the Lords by then. (*He hangs up.* JOHNSON *enters and announces* WILFRED OLIVER, *who comes in, then* JOHNSON *exits.* OLIVER *is a very attractive, somewhat epicene American, about thirty-five years old*) Well, my dear Wilfred, how are you?

OLIVER Lovely to see you, Lord Pengo.

PENGO Too bad about the play.

OLIVER (*Winces*) Rotten luck. When once I do get a good part, the critics say the play is lousy. Actually, I was miscast.

PENGO (*Genially, as if to cheer him up*) A mediocre actor is always miscast!

OLIVER (*Bitterly*) That's very kind of you!

PENGO As you know, my dear Wilfred, I am very fond of you. Have the highest regard for you—but not as an actor. What are your plans?

OLIVER Look for another job.

PENGO How would you like to come back to work for me?

OLIVER Well, to tide me over. But, as I made clear the last time I worked for you, my heart is in the theatre.

PENGO You should get a more responsive sweetheart, dear boy. Face the facts. You are good-looking, charming, you've nice manners and a really extraordinary taste in furniture and decoration. That's your true talent. If you take my advice, my dear Wilfred, before long you'll be in a position, if you still want it, to have your own theatre.

OLIVER (*His eyes alight*) If I thought I could do that. . .

PENGO Why not? There are more ways than one of reaching your objective, my boy.

OLIVER (PENGO *has him*) First step?

PENGO You sail for home Wednesday on the *Mauretania.* (*At his telephone*) I'll get you a lovely cabin. (*Into the phone*) Book an outside cabin "A" deck, Mr. Wilfred Oliver, *Mauretania*, Wednesday. I know all about its being sold out. Call Jackson. It's a must. Give me Vickers. (*A moment*) Vickers, Wilfred Oliver comes back with us, as of today. Double his last salary. He'll be down directly for an advance. (*With a happy smile to* OLIVER) What *was* your last salary, Wilfred?

OLIVER (*Laughs*) You're wonderful, Joe.

PENGO (*Beams at him*) Aren't you being familiar?

OLIVER I got so I called you Joe.

PENGO Perfectly all right, my boy. But never before a customer. Especially never before an American customer. They dearly love a Lord. By the way, Wilfred . . .

OLIVER Yes, my Lord?

PENGO There'll be a charming fellow American on the *Mauretania*—Mrs. Enoch Drury. (WILFRED *is impressed. He emits a long, low whistle*) She used to be on the stage—bond between you. Also, she is thinking of building a house on Fifth Avenue . . .

OLIVER Oh?

PENGO Which will, I hope, make another bond between you. I rely on you to furnish it, my boy, with the best Pengos, so that when I come to dine, I'll feel perfectly at home! (*He enjoys this conceit. He is in high fettle. He starts walking* WILFRED *out. He buzzes for* JOHNSON) You understand, my boy . . .

OLIVER Yes?

PENGO The connection, as before, will be unofficial.

OLIVER Quite.

PENGO Preferable that no one knows you are on my payroll.

OLIVER Quite.
        (JOHNSON *comes in*)

JOHNSON You rang, my Lord?

PENGO Johnson, take Mr. Oliver to the Chinese Gallery.

JOHNSON Yes, my Lord. (*As he goes out with* OLIVER *in tow*) I thought you might be interested to know, my Lord . . .

PENGO Yes, Johnson?

JOHNSON On her way to the Chinese Gallery, Mrs. Drury noticed the Red Boy of Goya. She fell madly in love with him.

PENGO (*With a gleam*) Good. I encourage all love affairs that take place in my premises.
   (*He gives* OLIVER *a look which* OLIVER *understands. As* JOHNSON *and* OLIVER *leave,* DEREK *enters*)

DEREK What's Oliver doing around here?

PENGO I have just rehired him. He's working for us again. (*Sees that* DEREK *is displeased*) I know you don't like him, Derek, but the world's full of people one doesn't like. Do you suppose I like my clients? With very few exceptions—no. And do you suppose they like me? Most of them can't bear me. They deal with me because they have to. (PENGO *sits at his desk, going over one memo after another with tremendous concentration and signing them. At the same time he is talking to* DEREK. PENGO *picks up a letter and glances at it*) Mrs. Bovington. From Palm Beach. She misses me.

DEREK Who's Mrs. Bovington?

PENGO One of the most important widows in America!

DEREK Rather an odd classification.

29

PENGO Don't you know, my boy, that the widows *own* America? Their husbands die prematurely of exhaustion getting it for them. (*He signs the last memo, gets up, goes to the Allendale and stands before it in an ecstasy of contemplation*) Look at it, my boy, look at it! Have you ever seen anything so stupendous, so overpowering, so . . .

DEREK You seem to forget, Dad—I'm not a customer!

PENGO It's a miracle.

DEREK It *is* beautiful.

PENGO (*Wheels around*) You misunderstand. The fact that I own it—*that's* the miracle.

DEREK You won't own it long.

PENGO I'll own it forever.

DEREK (*Teasing him*) Can you afford it?

PENGO In my own mind, I consider that I merely lease my pictures to my customers. After I'm gone, you'll write my life, Derek, and you'll make clear that I have done pioneer work. I have made the Americans art-conscious.

DEREK Who's writing this biography—you or me?

PENGO But it's true! Look at *me*—I have been exalted by my merchandise. I want the Americans to be exalted by it too.

DEREK You certainly make them pay through the nose for it!

PENGO Only for art, dear boy. The exaltation is free!
(*With a last look at the Allendale*) Terrific! Terrific!

DEREK You're constantly selling, aren't you? If not to your
customers—to yourself!

PENGO What's wrong with selling? The Americans have
made it the universal pastime . . . And speaking of
selling—it becomes my unpleasant duty to reprimand
you. For your own good, you understand!

DEREK I know! It'll hurt you more than it hurts me!

PENGO It does, as a matter of fact. You lost me the sale of
the Houdon bust to Bingham. I instructed you to ask
fifty thousand dollars for it.

DEREK (*Shamefacedly*) I did!

PENGO No, you didn't. Johnson was present and he told
me. You kept saying fi-fi-fi- —you couldn't seem to get it
out.

DEREK It seemed an awful lot to ask.

PENGO Anyone to whom fifty thousand dollars seems to
be a lot of money shouldn't be working for me!

DEREK That's what I keep telling you, Dad. I *shouldn't*
be working for you.

PENGO (*Soothing him*) No harm done. I'll sell it to some
other American for sixty. But practice, Derek, practice.
Keep saying fifty thousand dollars, fifty thousand dollars,
over and over to yourself till it comes naturally.

DEREK It's no good, Father. I'll never get used to it. You'd better fire me.

PENGO Can't. Your mother would never forgive me. (VICKERS, *a dried-up, fussy, anxious little accountant, enters. He carries some financial statements*) Well, Vickers—how are we?

VICKERS Thank you, your Lordship . . .
(*He looks unhappily at* DEREK)

DEREK Hello, Vickers.

VICKERS How do you do, Mr. Derek?

DEREK I have a feeling Vickers would rather see you alone, Father.

PENGO Not at all. Why should he? (*To* VICKERS) It's all going to belong to Derek one day, Vickers, and the more he learns about the facts of life in art, the better.

VICKERS (*Coughs*) The fact is, my Lord . . .

PENGO Yes, Vickers?

VICKERS The fact is—to put it bluntly—we are overextended!

PENGO (*As if surprised*) Are we, Vickers?

VICKERS Very much. We have bank notes coming due, here in London alone, within the next four months . . . (*He pauses impressively*) to the tune of one million four hundred thousand pounds!

PENGO Four months is a long time. A lot may happen in four months.

VICKERS (*Pessimistically*) Sincerely trust that it does, your Lordship.

PENGO (*To* DEREK) Vickers always tells me what I owe other people. He never tells me what other people owe me.

VICKERS I am aware of that, your Lordship.

PENGO What do they owe me in America, Vickers? What, for example, does Phineas D. Terwilliger owe me?

VICKERS Seven hundred and fifty thousand pounds, your Lordship.

PENGO (*Teasing him*) Don't you think he's good for it? The richest man in the world (*With a wink to* DEREK) . . . though I have several clients who are richer!

VICKERS If you will forgive me, your Lordship—it is not a question of Mr. Terwilliger's solvency, but of your own.

PENGO (*Doesn't like this*) Nonsense. In America alone . . .

VICKERS Our American outstandings will more than meet our obligations—if you collect them. But you never ask for money, your Lordship. You let them hold on to our inventory forever. Millions in capital tied up. And you go on spending.

PENGO (*Conscious of* DEREK *as an audience*) Can't talk to my American clients about money. It would be undignified. Besides, the subject bores me.

VICKERS We'd be all right—if only you stopped buying!

PENGO   Then what will I sell?

VICKERS   (*His voice rises; it is an old issue between them*)
Your basement. Liquidate your basement. It's full of
stuff. Get rid of it.

PENGO   Why is it in the basement? Because I *couldn't* get
rid of it.

VICKERS   Sell it to another dealer. Sell it to Heimler's.

PENGO   And let Heimler's establish a reputation on *my*
basement? (*With dignity*) They may be in the basement, Vickers, but they're still Pengos.

VICKERS   (*His voice rises in a wail of pleading*) If you'd
only stop buying new stuff . . .

PENGO   (*Can't resist*) What I buy is very *old* stuff.

VICKERS   If you'd only stop buying anything—just for six
months—I might be able to strike a trial balance. Forgive
me, your Lordship, but this time the situation is really
serious. I can't sleep nights worrying that the banks will
call our loans. If you'd only hold in for six months!

PENGO   (*To soothe him;* VICKERS *is really in a state*) All
right, Vickers, I'll try.

VICKERS   (*Turns to* DEREK *for help*) You see the point,
don't you, Mr. Derek?

DEREK   Of course I do, Vickers. But you know Father—
he's incorrigible.

VICKERS   (*Sweating*) I would appreciate your help, Mr.
Derek.

DEREK I'll do what I can . . .

VICKERS Forgive me, your Lordship, for speaking so
frankly. I felt it was my duty.

PENGO Of course, Vickers, I understand perfectly. I'll try
to do better.

VICKERS It is of the utmost importance, I assure you.
Lately, I've been at my wit's end. If you don't stop spending I shall never be able to make a respectable trial
balance. It will kill our credit. Good morning, your Lordship.

PENGO Thank you, Vickers. (VICKERS *goes out.* PENGO
looks after him, meditatively) You would think, to
listen to Vickers, that all I exist for is to help him with a
trial balance. A *respectable* trial balance. What would
be an *illicit* trial balance? What?

DEREK Well, he has a point, you know.

PENGO Of course he has a point. Admirable fellow, Vickers. Been with me since my father's day. But let me tell
you something about Vickers, and *all* comptrollers.
They're right ninety-nine percent of the time; but on
that remaining one percent, that one percent when
they're wrong and I'm right—on that one percent—*I live.*
          (JOHNSON *comes in with a cable*)

JOHNSON Cable, my Lord.

PENGO (*Rips the cable open as* JOHNSON *goes out; apoplectic*) Damn!

DEREK What's the matter?

PENGO It's gone astray.

DEREK What has?

PENGO Cosmo Prince's ballroom.

DEREK Have you mislaid it?

PENGO I bought him a Renaissance ballroom out of the Lamballe Palace in Rome. Had the whole thing shipped —down to the last doorknob. (*Taps the cable furiously*) And now it's got lost somewhere in transit.

DEREK Insufficient postage, perhaps.
    (*By this time* PENGO *is at the telephone*)

PENGO It's no joke, Derek. Cosmo Prince is the most important press lord in America. Very impatient man when he doesn't get what he wants. (*Into the phone*) Get me Burgess. (*Continues to* DEREK) Moreover, he's giving a big ball at his ranch in California and he wants a proper room to give it in. (*He's got Burgess*) Burgess, I just had a cable. Cosmo Prince's ballroom is lost in transit. What about it? (*A moment;* PENGO *is very angry*) If you know what's good for you, Burgess, you'll trace that ballroom!
    (*He bangs the telephone down*)

DEREK (*Tense, making a supreme effort*) Father, I . . . I've got to talk to you.

PENGO Well, aren't we?

DEREK I mean—about myself. I've been on the verge of telling you for a long time but I never get the chance to talk to you.

PENGO (*Somewhat impatient*) Well, what is it? What do you want to tell me?

DEREK The fact is . . . I'm unhappy. I don't want to sell. I'm not a salesman.

PENGO With the inventory I leave you and the money I leave you and the prestige I leave you—you won't have to be a salesman. A Pengo will be its own trademark.

DEREK I'll never be able to succeed you, Dad. It's like a great physician who leaves his practice to a son who hasn't got the bedside manner. I'm so torn, Dad.

PENGO What about?

DEREK It's hard for me to say . . . (*Smiles at his father*) I've acquired the English restraint. But, after all, we are Hungarians, aren't we? You were born there, so why shouldn't I say that . . . I'm so very fond of you—in fact I—

PENGO You adore me. Say it right out—as if it were fifty thousand dollars!

DEREK (*Does come out with it*) Yes. I do. At the same time . . .

PENGO Come out with it. What is it?

DEREK There are times . . . when I'm ashamed of you. I suffer for you. I hear things about you . . .

PENGO Certainly. I know.

DEREK You clown so, Dad. You amuse these people, I know; but you make yourself a clown to do it.

PENGO   It's my passport to their society. Why should they put up with me if I don't entertain them? I am not ambitious to be one of them. Not at all. I feel I have to pay my way, by amusing them!

DEREK   Court jester!

PENGO   Very good, Derek. Couldn't be better put!

DEREK   Look, Dad—you've got the most beautiful pictures in the world. Why don't you let them sell themselves? Why do you have to exploit them, and yourself, the way you do?

PENGO   *I* know I've got the most beautiful pictures in the world, you know it, Berenson knows it—but the Americans don't know it!

DEREK   Why must you employ people like Wilfred Oliver?

PENGO   (*Making a face*)   He's a nice fellow.

DEREK   He's not a nice fellow.

PENGO   He's useful.

DEREK   Why don't you employ him openly then? The secret payroll: butlers, maids, valets . . .

PENGO   They all do it, my boy, even my most respectable rivals. It's a trade technique.

DEREK   I hate it—the whole technique. You make charlatans out of the pictures.

PENGO   (*Equably*)   How?

DEREK   By sensationalizing them. Always getting them

into the papers—and yourself. You talk too much—in public and private. Why don't you keep quiet?

PENGO Do you want me to be like my customers, who never say a word?

DEREK Let the pictures speak for you!

PENGO Most of my pictures are Italian. They don't speaka da English! (*Appeals to him*) Don't you want me to have any fun, my boy? Do you grudge me a little fun? (*Goes to door—speaks to* JOHNSON, *who is offstage*) Johnson, will you please ask Mrs. Drury to detach herself from her party. I wish to speak to her alone for a moment.

JOHNSON (*Offstage*) Yes, my Lord.

DEREK That's what *I* want, but I never seem to get the chance!

PENGO What?

DEREK To speak to you alone for a moment!

PENGO Something worrying you?

DEREK A lot.

PENGO What is it? The Drury girl? Daphne?

DEREK That's part of it.

PENGO You know, Derek, I wish you'd marry a less complicated girl. Also . . .

DEREK Well?

PENGO   Her father would be furious. I'd lose all chance to get him as a customer.

DEREK   Everything for selling . . .

PENGO   I believe I made a mistake, Derek, when I sent you to an English public school. They don't evidently teach you the facts of life.

DEREK   Dad! There's something—terribly important to me —that I've been hiding from you—that I've simply got to talk to you about.

PENGO   What is it?

DEREK   I can't just blurt it out—it's too personal. You've got to give me time.

PENGO   On the boat—we'll have plenty of time on the boat.

DEREK   On the boat you'll be selling dull eighteenth-century portraits to Brink.

PENGO   (*Casually, enjoying the little surprise*)   Do you call the Blue Boy of Gainsborough dull?

DEREK   (*Astonished*)   But you don't own the Blue Boy.

PENGO   (*With a wide smile at him*)   No, but I will. After I've sold it to Brink—I'll buy it! (DEREK *can't help laughing*)   That's the spirit, my boy. Have fun! I have fun.

DEREK   I know you do, but all the same, I have an awful feeling, Dad. That one day—that this can't keep up—that one day—you'll come a cropper.

PENGO How is it that an optimist like myself should have a pessimist for a son? Get it from your mother, I expect. (*He is now at his desk, picks up a photograph of Lady Pengo*) You know, Derek, from the beginning, if I'd listened to your mother . . . Have you seen this new photograph? Isn't she lovely?

DEREK (*Looking at the photograph*) I love that photograph. Mother complains about you, you know—she never sees you.

PENGO (*Staring at the photograph*) I've got plans for that too, my boy. One day—one day . . . I'll buy a beautiful place somewhere and we'll settle down and live happily, forever . . .

(PRIMROSE *comes in*)

PRIMROSE (*In ecstasy*) Joe, I'm just in love with that Goya—that darling little Red Boy!

PENGO He is a darling, isn't he? And I'm about to sell Wally the Blue Boy. If you marry Wally, Prim, you'll have 'em both.

PRIMROSE I don't like the Blue Boy. He's wishy-washy.

PENGO I love you, Prim, because you know what you like.

PRIMROSE And what do you think, Joe? That nice Mr. Oliver, I just met, he's sailing too.

PENGO Oh, is he?

PRIMROSE He's charming.

PENGO Yes, charming. But he knows it! Exquisite taste

in furniture and decoration but not much else. A light-weight, really.

PRIMROSE (*To* DEREK) Oh, Derek, I just spoke to Daphne . . . she says yes she'll have dinner with you. You're to pick her up at Prince's Gate.

DEREK Fine.
(*He goes out*)

PRIMROSE When's Drury coming, Joe?

PENGO Any minute.

PRIMROSE I'm so nervous I can't stand it. Haven't seen him for three years and four months. S'pose he cuts me? Capable of it, you know. He's a cold man—on the surface anyway.

PENGO I'll see you through it. Shall I leave you alone with him?

PRIMROSE (*Panicked*) Don't do that. I just want to see him—see how he acts.

PENGO (*To change the subject*) Derek seems to have your daughter considerably on his mind.

PRIMROSE I know.

PENGO Is he at all on *her* mind?

PRIMROSE Daphne tells me she loves Derek.

PENGO (*Shrewdly*) Is that encouraging?

PRIMROSE She's a funny girl, Daphne. I just don't under-stand her way of lovin'. While she's lovin' she's lookin' somewhere else to see what's cookin' in another direction. She's got pretty feet but she's never swept off 'em. When I was her age, I was sure swept off mine.

PENGO Derek better get over it.

PRIMROSE Feel kinda sorry for the boy. Afraid Daphne'll make him suffer.

PENGO Oh well, we all go through that when we're young, I suppose.

PRIMROSE Wouldn't mind that if you could get over it when you're older! That's what my analyst keeps tellin' me. Dr. Jerome Auerbach.

PENGO Oh, I know Dr. Auerbach. What does he tell you?

PRIMROSE Stop hangin' around waitin' for Drury to come back, he keeps tellin' me.

PENGO Sound advice.

PRIMROSE If I divorced him, I'd have to give up Daphne. Wouldn't be good for Daphne. Besides, I hate divorce. Hate the idea of being a divorced woman.

PENGO Venture to say you wouldn't be in that position for long.

PRIMROSE That's the trouble.

PENGO What do you mean?

PRIMROSE Oh, Joe, you know, I'm so romantic. With my nature, I'm afraid if I were free I'd do something silly. And so would Enoch. That tramp who's got her hooks on him would get him.

43

PENGO   What happened between you and Drury anyway? Was it ever any good?

PRIMROSE   For a few years it was. I was so young when he married me. I was so flattered. Imagine, Joe. Imagine what it meant for a girl like me—worked since I was a kid in a vaudeville act—married to a man who had a whole town named after him. Drury, Illinois. And I was to be Mrs. Drury. Mrs. Drury, Illinois.

PENGO   Was Drury, Illinois, gay?

PRIMROSE   That's what it wasn't! I had such plans. What I was going to do in the town—get friendly with the people, and do things for them. But when I got there I found that everybody in Drury hated Drury and that Drury hated them. And there'd be strikes and Enoch hired people who went out and—well, there'd be shooting. And that house we lived in—that great, silent house we lived in. Enoch always in conference with other silent men. Oh, it was awful!

PENGO   Then why do you cling to it?

PRIMROSE   Because I'm sorry for him. Funny thing is, he wants to be loved too. People say he's cold; he ain't really, he's stubborn. Take his political ambitions; he's always nominated, never elected. (*A moment*) Joe, will you promise me something?

PENGO   Anything at all.

PRIMROSE   If you ever get a chance, Joe . . .

PENGO   Yes, my dear?

PRIMROSE If you ever get close to him—the way *you* do to people . . .

PENGO Not likely with him.

PRIMROSE Well, if you do . . .

PENGO Yes?

PRIMROSE (*Simply*) Tell him I worship him, will you?

PENGO Why don't you tell him yourself?

PRIMROSE Haven't got the nerve. (*Smiles fondly at him*) Joe, I wish you were sailing.

PENGO Be there in three weeks.

PRIMROSE We've got to talk over the plans for the house. Do you think I should build the house?

PENGO Definitely. That hotel of yours is depressing.

PRIMROSE Kind of afraid I'll rattle around in a big house. Without a man—what good is a house?

PENGO You've been alone too much, Prim. You've been brooding too much. Because your marriage to Drury was a failure you think of yourself as a failure. It's ridiculous. I'll fill your house with the best people—and the best pictures.

PRIMROSE You cheer me up, Joe, you really do!

PENGO The Red Boy will cheer you up even more.

PRIMROSE Hope you're not going to make me pay too much for him.

45

PENGO My dear Primrose, if I don't make you pay a lot for him you won't respect him!

PRIMROSE (*Delighted*) You kill me, Joe. You really do!
(JOHNSON *comes in*)

JOHNSON Mr. Drury is downstairs, my Lord.

PENGO A moment, Johnson. I'll buzz.
(JOHNSON *goes. The effect on* PRIMROSE *is devastating. She is in a flutter*)

PRIMROSE I can't do it. I can't. If he acted—you know—cold—it'd break me up.

PENGO Why don't you go downstairs and just run into him—accidentally?

PRIMROSE I just can't. How do you get out of here?

PENGO (*He is at a small door to the left, which he opens for her*) Through here.

PRIMROSE (*Runs to the door*) I'm a mess, Joe. I don't know whether I'm comin' or goin'.
(*She runs out.* PENGO *shuts the door after her. He goes into action, buzzes for* FILBERT, *who comes in at once*)

PENGO Filbert. Drape the Allendale. (FILBERT *arranges a velvet curtain to cover the Allendale*) All right, Filbert. Tell Johnson to show Mr. Drury in.
(PENGO *gets a firm grip on himself. His lips murmur adulatory phrases.* JOHNSON *comes in*)

JOHNSON (*Ushering in* MR. DRURY) Mr. Enoch Drury.
(JOHNSON *goes.* ENOCH DRURY *is elegant, aloof, pa-*

trician. He has a noble head and an astringent voice)

PENGO *(Advancing to* DRURY*)* I am happy to see you again, Mr. Drury.

DRURY Thank you.
(They do not shake hands)

PENGO Would you like a drink—a cup of tea perhaps?

DRURY I am afraid I am pressed for time.

PENGO Actually I have to be at the House of Lords myself at three-thirty.

DRURY I should be pleased to see the Allendale. I know it is a beautiful picture. But I must advise you that if it is a Titian—I shan't be interested. I am well supplied with Titians.

PENGO Berenson certifies it as a Giorgione.

DRURY *(Coldly)* I have heard the contrary.

PENGO I shall satisfy you on that point, Mr. Drury. *(A pause.* DRURY *says nothing. Finally)* As I know how pressed you are for time, I had the Giorgione brought in here.

DRURY Thank you.

PENGO Won't you sit down while I show it to you properly?

DRURY Thank you.
*(*PENGO *pushes a beautifully brocaded armchair midstage before the Allendale.* DRURY *sits in it)*

47

PENGO   I may tell you, Mr. Drury, that since that greatest
of all masterpieces has come into my possession, I have
been unable to eat or sleep . . . There it is! Feast your
eyes upon it—the Allendale Giorgione. (DRURY *listens
to this impassively.* PENGO *shuts off the lights, leaving on
only the electrolier that lights the Allendale. A silence.*
PENGO *goes on—eloquent in a vacuum*)   It is not merely
a painting you will observe, Mr. Drury. What shall I
say? It is music. Colored music. (*He peers narrowly at*
DRURY *to see the effect. There is no effect.* DRURY *is
staring at some inner vision*)   This picture, I fondly believe, will confer immortality upon you, Mr. Drury.
People who have never heard of Giorgione will know
Enoch Drury. Your name will be linked in this life and
through eternity—*The Drury Giorgione!* (PENGO *peers
at* DRURY *again.* DRURY *remains impassive*)   A distin-
guished partnership, don't you think? (PENGO *hopes for
an answer.* DRURY *does not look as if he wanted to go into
partnership with anybody. There is no answer.* PENGO
*gives up and with a certain despair goes into the solemn
facts of biography*)   You know that Giorgione died
when he was thirty-two years old . . .

    (*Totally unaffected by this premature death,* DRURY
    *sits in stony silence. On this impasse the curtain
    slowly descends*)

ACT TWO

ACT TWO

Scene: LORD PENGO'S *art gallery in New York, five months later. It is a large, sumptuous room done in classic Greek Revival in several tones of gold and soft cream. The walls are covered in velvet. Up center is a pillared arch showing a large sky-lighted gallery. On the back wall of the gallery hangs a large portrait of Mrs. Siddons by Reynolds. On the right wall is Van Dyck's Henrietta Maria. On the left wall, downstage, we see the Masaccio which was visible in Act One. On the right, on a pedestal, is an exquisite bust of a little girl by Settignano. Between the pillars is an architect's model of an art museum. This model stands on a wheeled base. On the right, downstage, is a Renaissance throne on a dais. Over the throne is a pillared baldachino.*

At rise: MISS SWANSON, PENGO'S *American first secretary, is sitting at* PENGO'S *desk going over some memoranda.* MISS SWANSON *is a spinster of uncertain age, severely dressed, with her hair done up in a topknot. She has a sharp mind. She has been with* PENGO *for thirty years —is used to him—and is fascinated by him. She's known* DEREK *since he was an infant and adores him.* DEREK *walks in. He is in low spirits.*

MISS SWANSON (*Holds up an invoice and studies it pensively*) Now would you please tell me, Derek . . .
(DEREK *looks at her inquiringly*) Would you please tell

51

me how the noble Lord, your father, could make a Jewish hotel man from Chicago feel that he just had to have twelve madonnas?

DEREK Perhaps he's got a mother complex.

MISS SWANSON And for this highly restored Renaissance dame who couldn't have been so hot even *before* she was restored, Mr. Enoch Drury is paying four hundred and eighty-five thousand dollars.

DEREK That's reasonable!

MISS SWANSON The higher they are the harder they fall. It's really wonderful, Derek, to see your father operate on these boys. They're all jealous of Drury, you know. Especially Brink. Your father says to Brink: "My dear Wally, Drury may have the mountains, but you have the peaks." Then he tells Drury: "Brink may have the peaks, my dear Mr. Drury, but you have the mountains . . ."

DEREK Dad is certainly master of the reversible compliment.

MISS SWANSON You're not your usual bright self lately, dear boy. What's wrong?

DEREK Just about everything.

MISS SWANSON Your sweetheart's back in town, you should be oh-so-happy!

DEREK I'm oh-so-miserable.

MISS SWANSON Tell the Beatrice Fairfax of Fifty-seventh Street.

DEREK I'm in a false position. With Daphne, with my father, with this business—with everything. Chiefly with myself. No decision. No courage.

MISS SWANSON You promised me you'd tell your father about your secret ambition. That you don't want to sell pictures, that you want to paint them.

DEREK I've tried to tell him. Like the fif-fif-fifty thousand dollars, I couldn't get it out. Especially the kind of thing I want to paint. Can you imagine Father! You know how he hates modern painting.

MISS SWANSON I've shown your work to several of my emancipated art-critic friends. They say it shows originality and promise.

DEREK (*His face alight with pleasure—incredulously*) Did they? Did they really?

MISS SWANSON You seem surprised.

DEREK Well, I am. When I'm painting I'm happy but I struggle with uncertainty. Half the time I think I'm crazy—presumptuous—to think that I could ever be an artist. What you tell me—and I know you wouldn't say it if it weren't true—is reassuring . . . It's the first encouragement I've had. It's welcome.

MISS SWANSON There's enough there to convince *me*.

DEREK You know, Miss Swanson, I have been spoon-fed on the most expensive paint in the world—it's beginning to choke me. I feel things differently from these people. I have got to find my own way to—

MISS SWANSON You're doomed to be an artist. Tell you

53

what, Derek! I'll give you a room in my mother's cottage in Glens Falls. Tell your father you're resigning and go up there and paint!

DEREK   I'd love to if Daphne came along.

MISS SWANSON   Can't see Daphne in Glens Falls. Not quite.

DEREK   That's not going so well either—with Daphne. She blows hot and cold. One day she's all lovey-dovey, the next day I can't get her on the telephone. There's something wrong. Have felt it lately. Truth is, Miss Swanson . . .

MISS SWANSON   What?

DEREK   I'm a misfit.

MISS SWANSON   So are most artists. That's what makes them artists.

DEREK   Father's overwhelming. Just as I'm most angry with him—

MISS SWANSON   He becomes so enchanting or so funny that you forgive him.

DEREK   Yes.

MISS SWANSON   I've been up against that for years! It would be a private revenge for me in a way if you stood up to him. I love the irony of it—that he, who buys up modern pictures to hide them away in his basement so his clients won't get used to them, should find himself fathering them . . . You take the bull by the horns and tell him.

DEREK It's not easy. When I tell him I admire modern paintings, he hits the ceiling. "What, those detached eyes swimming in tomato sauce? You admire those?" It dries me up.

MISS SWANSON You've just got to do it.

DEREK He'll have a fit.

MISS SWANSON He sure will. Oh boy, how I'll tease him!

DEREK Well, Miss Swanson, you give me courage. I'll tell him the dark secret. Where is Father?

MISS SWANSON With Sir William Fitzpatrick planning Primrose's great mansion. And speaking of romance, how is that oh-so-exquisite Wilfred Oliver getting along with doll Primrose?

DEREK She dotes on him. Poor Prim—I'm worried about her.

MISS SWANSON Why? She's having fun, isn't she? What's wrong with that?

DEREK She's gone head-over-heels—she hasn't got a chance against that sleazy Don Juan.

MISS SWANSON Do you think he'll get her to marry him?

DEREK Of course he will—she's vulnerable—he's nimble. What a windfall! Luxury cruise, all expenses paid. Rather makes me sick, you know.

MISS SWANSON Why?

DEREK What's Dad running anyway? An art gallery or a matrimonial agency?

MISS SWANSON   That's just what I asked your father . . .

DEREK (*Amused*) Dad will take anything from you! What did he say?

MISS SWANSON   "The point is, Miss Swanson," he said, "*we're selling!*" With him it's a kind of disembodied activity—like praying! (*She holds up another invoice*) Oh, boy! Oh, boy! Oh, boy!

DEREK   What's that?

MISS SWANSON   Invoice to Walter Cannon Brink, the Third. If I had that money . . . if I had a hundredth part of that money . . .

DEREK   What would *you* do with it, Miss Swanson?

MISS SWANSON   I wouldn't be spending it on lousy eighteenth-century English portraits!
   (PENGO *has come in and hears this*)

PENGO (*In wonderful humor*) Really, Miss Swanson! Now really! What language! Lousy: awful American word. You know you are the only American employed here. Don't you think, Derek, it was a mistake?

MISS SWANSON   I know your linguistic standards are high, Joe. Nothing but the purest French-Hungarian-Cockney spoken here.

PENGO   I'm afraid I'll have to fire you for that remark, Miss Swanson. I haven't the heart to do it. Derek, you'll have to do it.

MISS SWANSON   Come, come, Joe, those Englishmen in

cutaways you've got downstairs bore the pants off you. You know they do!

PENGO   At least, Miss Swanson, you might respect the pictures.

MISS SWANSON   What! Those eighteenth-century aunts and uncles and nieces! (*To* DEREK)   Brink the Third bought thirty-eight relatives of forgotten eighteenth-century aristocrats. Why doesn't he have his own relatives painted and hang *them*?

PENGO   It is obvious, Miss Swanson, that you haven't seen Brink's relatives.

MISS SWANSON   (*Gets up to go; takes a sheaf of invoices with her*)   By the way, Joe . . .

PENGO   Yes, Miss Swanson?

MISS SWANSON   Cosmo Prince called up from California. He's fit to be tied.

PENGO   What's wrong?

MISS SWANSON   That globe-trotting ballroom you sold him hasn't turned up yet!
     (PENGO *is very angry. He grabs a telephone*)

PENGO   (*Into the phone*)   Cable London. Burgess is fired. And trace that ballroom in twenty-four hours or the same will happen to you!

MISS SWANSON   (*At the door*)   Poor Cosmo. He's only got ninety rooms. Guess he'll have to give that ball in the privy!
     (*She goes out*)

PENGO (*Suddenly moody*) Miss Swanson goes too far.

DEREK I've just left Mother. She's awfully miffed with you, Dad.

PENGO (*Innocent surprise; he knows perfectly well what for*) Really? She was her usual sweet self last night at dinner. (*He picks up the Settignano Head of a Little Girl and adores it*) How do you like this little girl, Derek?

DEREK She's exquisite.

PENGO Saving her for your mother's birthday.

DEREK Oh, good! She'll love it!

PENGO Your mother always wanted a girl—in addition to you, of course. Well, here she is . . . What's your mother miffed with me about?

DEREK About Wetmore. The best butler she ever had, she says. You fired him.

PENGO (*With a twinkle*) On the contrary—I've promoted him!

DEREK Have you? To what?

PENGO (*With an effulgent, loving smile*) I've placed him with Enoch Drury.

DEREK (*Astonished*) At Drury's! No!

PENGO Yes, indeed. He's there now. It will be useful, Derek. Can't tell you how secure it makes me feel to have Wetmore at Drury's.

DEREK With Wetmore at Drury's you'll know instantly

58

which of your rivals will have the effrontery to show
their wares to the great man.

PENGO   You begin to show promise! Too bad your mother's
upset. Your mother's a wonderful woman, Derek, but in-
clined to be petty. This little Settignano'll make it up
to her!

(MISS SWANSON *comes in*)

MISS SWANSON   Sorry to interrupt. The *New York Herald*
just called. Bad news, Joe.

PENGO   (*Irritably*)   Well?

MISS SWANSON   Scotus B. Slemp is dead.

PENGO   (*Devastated*)   No! Can't be. Saw him yesterday.

MISS SWANSON   Nevertheless, he's gone. The paper wants
a statement.

PENGO   Two million dollars' worth of my stuff on consign-
ment to him . . .

MISS SWANSON   I know . . .

PENGO   (*With mounting indignation*)   Dawdled and dawdled . . . haggled and haggled . . . Wouldn't make up
his mind . . .

MISS SWANSON   As his heirs don't like you, it'll all come
back here.

PENGO   Raphael's Madonna . . .

MISS SWANSON   She'll come back! What about the statement?

PENGO (*Furious*) You see, Derek, what fools my clients are? Statement! Statement! Had Slemp not been niggardly I could give them a statement. I could say Scotus B. Slemp died owning one of the greatest pictures in the world, Raphael's Alba Madonna. Now what is there to say about him?

MISS SWANSON You might say he just barely missed owning Raphael's Alba Madonna.

PENGO (*Glares at her*) We are not amused, Miss Swanson!

MISS SWANSON After all, Joe, Slemp didn't die just to annoy you!

PENGO What do they think, these fellows—that they're eternal? This is serious.

MISS SWANSON (*Wearily*) They want a statement.

PENGO Get that educated librarian of mine, what's-his-name—McGiveny—to write it. Don't bother me.

MISS SWANSON I'll try.

PENGO (*Shouts*) You're fired, Miss Swanson. Get yourself another job!

MISS SWANSON Thank you, my Lord. Buzz me if you want me.
(*She goes out*)

PENGO (*In a brown study, muses*) Who can I sell the Raphael to? Do you know how much I paid Lady Desborough for it? Three-quarters of a million. There are

not many, Derek . . . not many who'll pay . . . How
stupid of Slemp! He'll never forgive himself!

DEREK (*Can't help laughing*) Oh, Dad!

PENGO (*Smiles ruefully*) In heaven, I mean! You see,
Derek, you see what I'm up against. I'm in a relay race.

DEREK How do you mean?

PENGO With death . . .

DEREK (*Concerned*) Aren't you well, Father?

PENGO Well, I'm not as young as I used to be. And neither are my clients. I spent a million dollars on this
building for a dozen customers. When I barged into
the American market there were three greats: Morgan,
Altman, the elder Widener. They all died on me.

DEREK Bad form!

PENGO They died on the pictures. They could all have
done better. My clients are so rich and powerful they
think they'll live forever. They are mistaken, as Scotus
B. Slemp has just demonstrated. After Morgan, Altman
and Widener died, I got three more, and they all died
on me too. And now there are Drury, Terwilliger, Brink
—all aging—and all cautious. I tell you, Derek, they
drive me crazy with their hesitations.

DEREK I don't see why you go on with it. Surely you've
made enough money by now.

PENGO That shows how little you understand me—if you
think it's money I'm after.

DEREK What then?

PENGO (*All this time he has been thinking of the Raphael; suddenly, with the illumination of a problem miraculously solved*) Of course, Derek! Of course!

DEREK Of course what?

PENGO Drury—Drury must buy the Raphael! (*Darts to the phone*) Get me Wetmore. (*Hangs up*) What a lucky break for Drury—Slemp popping off like that! To those that hath, Derek, shall be given. Lucky Drury!

DEREK (*Desperate to get him back to personal relations*) Outside of your business, you haven't an interest in the world. Look at your relations with Mother.

PENGO (*Bridling*) What's wrong with my relations with your mother? I'm a devoted husband. I never so much as look at another woman.

DEREK And you don't look at her, either. She was complaining to me only yesterday—you've been telling her for years: "Some day we'll live quietly and normally and happily." When is it coming, this perpetually receding "some day"?

PENGO (*Suddenly quiet*) When my Design is completed.

DEREK What design?

PENGO My Grand Design. (*The telephone rings;* PENGO *answers*) . . . Wetmore, I'd like very much to speak to Mr. Drury . . . something important has come up . . . Oh? . . . When will he be back? (PENGO's *voice rises somewhat*) Did he? . . . Did he really? . . .

Well, if he shouldn't come here, tell him I'm anxious to speak to him, will you? . . . Thank you, my boy. (PENGO *hangs up. He faces* DEREK *in triumph*) Wetmore says Drury may visit me here. We're going up in the world, Derek.

DEREK (*Insists*) What is your Grand Design?
（PENGO *goes to the model of the museum and lays his hand tenderly on it*)

PENGO This—by my pet American architect . . . Design for a national gallery—the ultimate destination of all my pictures—

DEREK (*Skeptically*) That's a noble objective!

PENGO It is my dream. I am grateful to my pictures. They've given me a career, a reason for existence— everything.

DEREK As I say—it's a noble objective. But is this altruism —unadulterated?

PENGO My dear boy, no motive is unadulterated. Still (*With a wave of his hand toward the glorified walls*) these pictures are my dependents and I must make some provision for them after my departure.
（FILBERT *comes in*)

FILBERT Cable, my Lord.
（PENGO *snatches it, rips it open.* FILBERT *goes*)

PENGO From Berenson.

DEREK What about?

63

PENGO (*As he studies the cable*) It's not a good day,
Derek!

DEREK The Allendale?

PENGO Listen. (*He reads the cable*) "It is true that I
once said the Allendale was a Giorgione. That was
thirty years ago. I am now convinced the picture was
by Titian—in fact, that it is the earliest known Titian.
I never stick to a mistake." (*He is apoplectic with rage*)
You see, Derek, what I'm up against! A mistake! He
calls it a mistake. The only sensible guess Berenson ever
made! A mistake! (*He picks up a heavy paperweight
and bangs it on glass-topped desk. He strides around
the room in a froth of anger*) Berenson crossing me up
like this! I tell you, Derek, Berenson may know what
is beautiful, but only I know what will sell! (*He finds
himself in front of the Masaccio*) This Masaccio! Berenson begged me to buy it. It's been hanging here forever, and no one buys it. It's gloomy. My clients don't
want gloomy pictures. Why should they? They're gloomy
themselves. They want color, beauty, and so do I. (*He
stares at it*) What is it, anyway? The Ascension, isn't
it?

DEREK No. The Circumcision.

PENGO That makes it worse! No wonder nobody buys
it. I'm sick of seeing it hanging there. I . . . (*He looks
at Berenson's cable again, crumples it and throws it
on the floor*) And now this mess over the Allendale.
Drury'll never buy it now. He doesn't want another
Titian. He wants a Giorgione.

Charles Boyer and Agnes Moorehead
as LORD PENGO and MISS SWANSON

Charles Boyer and Henry Daniell,
as LORD PENGO and ENOCH DRURY

DEREK It's a great picture—whether it's by Titian *or* Giorgione.

PENGO I've taught Drury—I've taught them all—to rely on Berenson's opinion. I've staked everything on Berenson's opinion.

DEREK It's like arguing whether Hamlet is by Shakespeare or Bacon. It's still Hamlet.

PENGO (*Shouts at him*) Look, Derek, if you don't see the difference between Giorgione and Titian, I'll tell you. It's a difference of four hundred thousand dollars. (*He taps the cable*) But the worst of it is, Drury will lose confidence in me. (*Paces about in agitated concentration—wheels about abruptly—struck by a new idea*) I wonder, Derek—

DEREK What?

PENGO Maybe I can sell the Allendale to Sylvester Schmitt.

DEREK I didn't know that Schmitt was interested.

PENGO Neither does he, but he'll find out. He was in here, you know, the other day.

DEREK Oh, was he?

PENGO You would have been very amused.

DEREK What's he like, Schmitt?

PENGO Well, you know he owns a thousand chain stores all over the United States. Used to buying things wholesale. Wanted to see things by the gross. Something about Schmitt—he can't resist a gross of anything. Well, I didn't have a gross, but I did pretty well. Filbert lugged in three Valesquezes, a Tintoretto, two Donatellos, three Houdon busts, and some tapestries I'd bought from King Alfonso of Spain. "How much for the lot?" he said. I named a dainty figure. Never had such a good time, Derek. Schmitt just sat there and glared at me.

DEREK   Did you land him?

PENGO   He got up stiffly and said he wasn't interested. I said I would save these things for him. "Don't save them, Lord Pengo," he said, "I'm not interested." Since then I hear he tells everybody I'm a robber and that he'll never set foot inside this place again.

DEREK   Then you didn't land him?

PENGO   On the contrary, I consider the things are sold. He is hovering, my boy—he is hovering on the abyss of commitment.

DEREK   I think I may trust you to push him over.

PENGO   But you don't realize what a character this man is! He's rich enough, if he wanted to, to charter the *Berengaria* and go around the world on it. And you know what he does with his evenings? Attends the Burton Holmes Travelogues. That's how he satisfies his wanderlust. And he saves the programs. Isn't it sweet? Very lonely man he is really (*The telephone rings;* PENGO *answers*) . . . as so many of these fellows are. Who? Oliver? (*At the mention of* OLIVER's *name,* DEREK *stiffens.* PENGO *has an instinct against talking to* OLIVER *in*

front of DEREK. *He knows* OLIVER *is a sore point with*
DEREK) Tell him I'll call him back.
  (*He hangs up*)

DEREK   Dad, I've never asked a favor of you before . . .

PENGO   Well?

DEREK   Fire Oliver. I beg you.

PENGO   Why are you so down on Oliver?

DEREK   Because he's a cynical opportunist.

PENGO   Life's full of 'em. Same might be said of me. Has
been.

DEREK   Oliver's not a good influence. He'll never make
Primrose happy. I feel it.

PENGO   You're naïve, Derek. You don't know these people.
They want romance. They want happiness and they
don't know how to get it. They want love.

DEREK   (*Scornfully*)   Love!

PENGO   Do you know what misery Primrose endured
when she was married to Drury? I do. If Oliver gives
her something to live for, if he makes her happy, then
he's *saving* her. What's your objection to it?

DEREK   Why do you have to mix in the private lives
of your clients?

PENGO   Because there's no other way. You forget, Derek,
I am an outsider fighting rivals who have been en-
trenched for generations. I have to invent my own

67

means, my own techniques. Show me another way and I'll follow it.

(FILBERT *comes in*)

FILBERT (*Announces*) Mr. Sylvester Schmitt.

PENGO (*Overjoyed and incredulous, but concealing it— casually to* FILBERT) Oh? I have no appointment with Mr. Schmitt.

FILBERT 'E apologizes for comin' without an appointment, but 'e says it's an emergency, my Lord.

PENGO Tell him I'll see him in a minute, Filbert. I am with an important client, but I'll see him directly. I'll buzz.

FILBERT Yes, my Lord.
(FILBERT *goes. The triumph of this softens* PENGO *immeasurably and sweeps his grievance out of his mind. He turns to* DEREK, *all tenderness*)

PENGO You see, Derek, I told you! They need me! They need me!

DEREK So do Mother and I, but we never seem to get you!

PENGO If you'll only be patient, both of you. Once my Grand Design goes through, I promise you, I'll buy you a villa in Italy—a château in France . . . (*With extravagant humor*) the Houses of Parliament.

DEREK I have no doubt you've put in a bid on them!
(PENGO *buzzes*)

PENGO Want to stay and watch me operate on Mr. Schmitt?

DEREK I'm afraid I'll cramp your style.

PENGO (*Quizzical*) Perhaps you would. . . .
(*As* DEREK *goes he passes the Settignano little girl. His hand caresses it*)

DEREK She *is* beautiful. Mother *will* love her.
(*He goes out.* FILBERT *ushers in* SYLVESTER SCHMITT. SCHMITT *is a large, towheaded bear of a man, about sixty, very phlegmatic; he moves lumberingly, as if even sitting down were a kind of commitment*)

PENGO (*Moves forward to greet him*) Mr. Schmitt! I am delighted to see you. Won't you sit down?

SCHMITT Just going to stay a minute.

PENGO (*Moves up a chair*) Why not be comfortable for that minute?

SCHMITT Why, thank you.
(*He heaves into the chair*)

PENGO I said I'd hold those glorious masterpieces you looked at the other day. I have kept my promise.

SCHMITT Told you last time, Lord Pengo, not interested. Unless . . .

PENGO There can be no change in the price I gave you.

SCHMITT Then forget about it. I came about something else.

69

PENGO You know, Mr. Schmitt, those works of art I showed you are beyond price. You are businessman enough to know, that no matter what you pay for the priceless, you're getting it cheap.

SCHMITT Don't want any bargains that cost that kind of money. I *work* for my money, Lord Pengo!

PENGO (*Easily*) Do you suggest that I don't? Do you think these works of art are easy to come by? Often they have to be pried away by main strength. It takes constant vigilance—and a great deal of capital—to acquire them. You get them only because *I* get them!

SCHMITT Not interested. (*His eye catches the Renaissance throne*) What's that fancy chair?

PENGO Not for sale.

SCHMITT (*Grumpy*) Then what's it doing here? In my stores, when I put things in the window, what would my customers say if I told them they were not for sale when they went in to buy them?

PENGO (*With quiet grandeur*) The throne is not in a window, Mr. Schmitt. (*He has taken a box of Havanas from his desk and now offers* SCHMITT *one*) Cigar?

SCHMITT Don't smoke.
    (*A silence*)

PENGO How's business, Mr. Schmitt?

SCHMITT My business is always good.

PENGO You are a lucky man. So many Americans com-

plain to me about the depression. Even Phineas D. Terwilliger the other day was telling me—

SCHMITT   No matter how poor people are they've always
got ten cents. I never charge more than ten cents.

PENGO   That is why, perhaps, you are disinclined to *pay*
more.

SCHMITT   (*Shoots him a suspicious look*)   What?

PENGO   Just a little joke.

SCHMITT   (*Wistfully*)   Joke. My wife tells me I got no
sense of humor.

PENGO   I'm sure she's wrong about that.
    (*A pause*)

SCHMITT   (*Finally*)   Fact is—that's why I came here—on
account of my wife.

PENGO   Really?

SCHMITT   We had a little fight.

PENGO   That happens.

SCHMITT   Wouldn't call it a fight exactly. Misunderstanding. More of a misunderstanding.

PENGO   Sometimes, Mr. Schmitt, those are worse than
fights.

SCHMITT   Yeah. Kind of makes me uncomfortable.

PENGO   I know what you mean. I quite sympathize. Fact

is—I am in exactly the same position at this moment—with *my* wife.

SCHMITT   Really?

PENGO   Afraid to go home—if you must know the truth.

SCHMITT   (*Gaining comfort by the instant*)   Really?

PENGO   I assure you!

SCHMITT   What are you doing tonight?

PENGO   I'll consult my calendar. (*Looks at his desk*)   My wife's giving a party at the Opera.

SCHMITT   (*Disappointed*)   Too bad!

PENGO   The Opera bores me.

SCHMITT   Ever hear a Burton Holmes Travelogue?

PENGO   No. I've often wanted to.

SCHMITT   Wonderful slides. Colored.

PENGO   Must be fascinating.

SCHMITT   Want to go with me tonight? I got two tickets —way down front.

PENGO   Delighted.

SCHMITT   It's going to be especially good tonight—it's the Holy Land!

PENGO   That should be very uplifting.

SCHMITT   Just what *I* thought. And I need to be uplifted. Will you have dinner with me?

PENGO   Afraid I can't do that.

SCHMITT   Then meet me at Carnegie Hall. In the lobby. Eight-thirty.

PENGO   I shall be there. (*A pause*)   Anything else I can do for you?

SCHMITT   Well, I thought if I could pick up something, some *little* thing, some little present—for my wife?

PENGO   We're in the same boat, aren't we? Just what I'm doing for *my* wife.

SCHMITT   (*Eagerly*)   What are you getting your wife?

PENGO   (*Goes to the Settignano*)   This lovely little girl by Settignano.

SCHMITT   Who?

PENGO   Florentine sculptor. Fifteenth century. Pupil of Donatello. Famous for his exquisite sculptures of women and children. Isn't she adorable?

SCHMITT   (*Suddenly greedy*)   My wife always wanted a girl.

PENGO   So did mine.

SCHMITT   My wife would like that.

PENGO   So would mine. (*His hand caresses the little girl tenderly*)   Look, Mr. Schmitt, this child is five hundred years old—and how fresh she is, how lit-up she is, how delicate, how eternally lovely she is.

SCHMITT (*Breaks into* PENGO's *reverie*) Listen, Pengo, what do you want for her?

PENGO Sorry. Not for sale. Now if you really want something handsome for your wife . . . (*He walks him to the sky-lighted gallery at the back and stands impressively before Sir Joshua Reynolds' Mrs. Siddons as the Tragic Muse*) Here is Sir Joshua Reynolds' portrait of Mrs. Siddons.

SCHMITT Who's Mrs. Siddons?

PENGO (*Gently*) The greatest English actress of the eighteenth century.

SCHMITT Matilda wouldn't like that.

PENGO Why not?

SCHMITT She wouldn't care to have me bring home an actress. She might think I'm playing around.

PENGO (*Moves away from Mrs. Siddons and stands before the Maria Theresa of Van Dyck*) Does Mrs. Schmitt's prejudice extend to queens? Here is Henrietta Maria by Van Dyck—the greatest Van Dyck I have ever owned . . . the best example of the great man at his best period.

SCHMITT (*Skeptically*) What makes it great?

PENGO The greatness of the artist. Look at it. Did you ever see such ravishing color?

SCHMITT Matilda's color-blind.

PENGO Van Dyck will cure her. What is more fitting than that you should present *your* queen—with another queen?

SCHMITT My wife's no queen. And she's color-blind. And she always wanted a little girl. We're childless, Lord Pengo. (*Goes back to the Settignano*) How much?

PENGO Not for sale.

SCHMITT (*Suddenly obsessed*) I've got to get her for my wife!

PENGO I have already promised her to mine.

SCHMITT Give *your* wife the Van Dyck.

PENGO (*Smiles*) Can't afford it. The Henrietta Maria is expensive.

SCHMITT If I buy this . . . this . . .

PENGO (*Supplies*) Settignano . . .

SCHMITT Yeah. If I buy her you'll be able to give the Van Dyck to your wife. How much is the Van Dyck?

PENGO Four hundred and seventy-five thousand dollars. You see, Mr. Schmitt, you'd have to buy several Settignanos.

SCHMITT (*In outrage*) Your prices, Pengo!

PENGO They are, I admit, Pengo prices. I also submit that you get for them—Pengo masterpieces.

SCHMITT Do you realize how many egg cups I have to sell to get four hundred and seventy-five thousand dollars?

75

PENGO I have absolute confidence in your ability to sell them. (*He leads him to the Masaccio*) Now here is a Masaccio. Bernard Berenson says it is an absolute masterpiece.

SCHMITT What is it?

PENGO It is called The Circumcision.

SCHMITT I don't like pictures of operations. (*Looks longingly at Settignano*) How much for this little girl?

PENGO (*Improvising*) One hundred and seventy-five thousand dollars.

SCHMITT I'll give you a hundred. Wrap her up and let me take her home. With her I can *go* home!

PENGO Sorry.

SCHMITT (*Desperate*) You got so much stuff here—can't you give your wife something else?

PENGO I might say the same of you. A thousand stores— haven't you got something in one of those thousand stores?

SCHMITT (*Literally*) My merchandise is standardized.

PENGO Ah, Mr. Schmitt, that is precisely where it differs from *my* merchandise!

SCHMITT (*Suffering*) One hundred and twenty-five thousand.

PENGO I implore you, for the sake of my domestic happiness, do not overpay me for this little Settignano. I implore you. Without her, I must confess to you, I won't dare go home.

SCHMITT   You don't have to go home. I'm taking you to the Holy Land.

PENGO   Even from the Holy Land, one must eventually return. Unless you are a Crusader, which I am not.

SCHMITT   One hundred and fifty.

PENGO   I don't want you to buy this, Mr. Schmitt. It would embarrass me greatly if you did. It would depress me.

SCHMITT   (*Vindictively*)   There's something about you, Lord Pengo . . .

PENGO   Yes, Mr. Schmitt?

SCHMITT   . . . that would make me very happy to depress you!

PENGO   Don't see why you are vindictive. After all—you're not my client yet.

SCHMITT   (*At his wit's end*)   I pay cash. Any reduction for cash?

PENGO   None whatever. You see, Mr. Schmitt, I am not short of cash. Are you?
       (SCHMITT *glares at him, takes a fountain pen and a checkbook out of his pocket and scribbles a check*)

SCHMITT   Wrap her up.
       (PENGO *buzzes.* FILBERT *comes in*)

PENGO   Mr. Schmitt has acquired this little Settignano. Will you take her down to Grandison please?

(FILBERT *lifts the head tenderly and starts to walk out with it*)

SCHMITT (*Offers the check to* PENGO)   Here you are, Pengo. Look at it.

PENGO (*Waves the check aside disdainfully*)   I believe I can trust you to make out a check, Mr. Schmitt. Filbert, will you take Mr. Schmitt's check please and give it to Vickers?

(FILBERT *takes* SCHMITT'S *check and goes*)

SCHMITT (*Aghast*)   What have I done?

PENGO   You may undo it in a moment. Say the word.

SCHMITT (*Lumbers up to his feet*)   Carnegie Hall. Eight-thirty.

PENGO   I look forward to it. You are very adroit, Mr. Schmitt. You see, you are able to go home—I am not!

SCHMITT (*Bitterly, as he goes*)   If anybody needs a trip to the Holy Land—*you do!*

(*The moment he is gone,* PENGO *executes a little pas de seul. He buzzes* DEREK'S *buzzer.* DEREK *comes back*)

PENGO (*Full of glee*)   Derek! You should have stayed—you should have stayed! What do you think I'm doing tonight? Mr. Schmitt is taking me to Burton Holmes.

DEREK   I thought we were going to the Opera.

PENGO   I leave it to you to explain to Mother.

78

DEREK   I am sure you do.

PENGO   By the way, Derek, something else I'd like you
to do for me . . .
   (*He is a little abashed and shamefaced by this one*)

DEREK   Yes?

PENGO   Go around to Cartier's, there's a good fellow, and
get something lovely for your mother. I rely on your
taste absolutely. Tell her I got it and sent it by you.

DEREK   Cartier's . . . I thought . . . (*He looks for the
Settignano, understands all*)   Dad! You didn't!

PENGO   (*Rueful*)   I didn't. Schmitt did!
   (DEREK *looks at him; his father looks so contrite he
has to laugh*)

DEREK   I hope you haven't already promised the Settignano to Mother. I hope she doesn't know about it!

PENGO   Unfortunately, I did and she does. That's the
trouble with me—too impulsive!

DEREK   Did you have to? Did you really have to? This
is the sort of thing you're always doing to Mother!

PENGO   What can I do, Derek? I'm weak. And you know
what these fellows are—so dictatorial. They badger me
till I give in!
   (*He gives* DEREK *a piteous, helpless smile, begging
for the sympathy that is the due of the persecuted.*
DEREK *almost gives it to him.* PENGO *puts his arm
around* DEREK'S *shoulder and starts with him out
of the room*)

The lights dim

79

ACT TWO

SCENE 2

Scene: At PENGO's. *Same afternoon.*

At rise: ENOCH DRURY's *elegant figure is moving from masterpiece to masterpiece, examining critically.* PENGO *is allowing* DRURY *to discover things for himself.*

PENGO You are the one client, Mr. Drury, who makes my job easy. I don't have to show you anything. You have your own eye.

DRURY *(Coldly)* Thank you. *(Just before he leaves the Van Dyck)* A quite fine Van Dyck. *(He moves on to Mrs. Siddons)* Reynolds. Very good. If I were collecting eighteenth-century English, I should acquire this.

PENGO Your taste, if I may say so, is impeccable.

DRURY *(Dryly)* I am quite aware, when you say that, that you are describing your own taste.

PENGO I cannot afford, if I am to supply you, to be less than impeccable.

DRURY *(Moving to the Masaccio)* My eye doesn't tell me what this is.

PENGO Masaccio. Berenson calls it a masterpiece. The Circumcision.

DRURY I am not interested in Jewish rites. (*Thinks perhaps this is tactless*) No offense, your Lordship.

PENGO Not at all. I understand prejudice. I have a few of my own. But Berenson says of this little picture—

DRURY Too dark. I like bright colors. (*He stands before the throne*) Renaissance?

PENGO Lorenzo de Medici's throne. (*Warms up*) It fires the imagination, doesn't it? There he sat, the magnificent Lorenzo; his captains reported to him, the admirals of his fleets. He dispensed largesse and justice—artist and ruler. You, Mr. Drury, are his spiritual descendant —a prince of the Renaissance, misplaced in time.

DRURY I've been reading about those fellows. They were lucky. (*With a wave toward the chair*) Lorenzo was lucky. (*With pensive reverie*) What a wonderful time he must have had! Those fellows—when they didn't like anybody, they just murdered them. No one thought anything about it. While I— You've seen the papers?

PENGO (*He has seen them*) I don't get time to read the papers.

DRURY Full of denunciation of me. Why? Because I was forced to call in strike-breakers to protect my property at my steel mills—which I had every right to do. I am disliked. I feel hostility around me.

PENGO Price of greatness.

DRURY I have done as much as any man to develop the industrial might of this country. I am denounced as a monopolist. I am. Monopoly is the course of evolution. I know more about the inner mechanism which makes this country tick than anybody alive. And yet—when I run for office—I am defeated.

PENGO   Democracy distrusts experts.

DRURY   That is true. You are not a fool, Pengo.

PENGO   Thank you. That is a compliment that can be paid to very few members of the House of Lords.
(DRURY *smiles frostily*)

DRURY   You are an amusing fellow. You are one of the very few I know—who entertains me. I don't make friends easily; why is it that I feel free to talk to you?

PENGO   Perhaps it is because we are not equals.

DRURY   After all, you *are* a member of the British House of Lords!

PENGO   I find that useful with the run of my American clients. It does not impress you!

DRURY   (*With a wan smile*)   I know England. I know how you wangled it!

PENGO   (*With a chuckle*)   You know because I told you!

DRURY   So you did! And a very funny story it was! The English are incorruptible, aren't they? You can't give them money. You've got to give them a check. (PENGO *laughs*. DRURY *goes on—with bitter sarcasm*)   And what about that exquisite connoisseur, Walter Cannon Brink? Is he buying anything?

PENGO   He's building a house.

DRURY   Is that because I am building one?

PENGO   Possibly.

DRURY   He imitates me in everything. Because I married Primrose, he wanted her. Because I started collecting, he did.

PENGO   In this mimicry—I encourage him.

DRURY   I am sure you do. (*Command to a court jester*) I love your stories, Pengo. Tell me one.

PENGO   (*Slips into the role easily*)   Well, just a few years ago, in London . . .

DRURY   Yes?

PENGO   The Duke of Lowtower—very High Church— asked me to look at an old master he was considering buying from Wellnew.

DRURY   Yes?

PENGO   "Very fine, your Grace," I said. "Very fine. But I suppose you are aware—those cherubs are homosexual." The old boy bristled and sent it back to Wellnew's like a shot.

DRURY   Well, you killed a sale for Wellnew . . .

PENGO   I did more than that, Mr. Drury.

DRURY   Did you?

PENGO   I acquired the picture and on those perverse cherubs I performed a remarkable feat of therapy.

DRURY   Did you restore the cherubs to normalcy?

PENGO Completely. Complete cure.

DRURY How?

PENGO By selling them to Phineas D. Terwilliger, in whose presence nobody could be perverse, and by doubling the price.

DRURY (*Amused*) Serves Terwilliger right—pompous ass. What an odd lot you deal with, Lord Pengo!

PENGO They are positively quaint!
(*A moment;* DRURY *gets up to go*)

DRURY Thank you very much, Lord Pengo, for a diverting half-hour.

PENGO Before you go, Mr. Drury—

DRURY Yes?

PENGO There is something very close to my heart—about which I have been meaning to speak to you for a long time.

DRURY (*On guard*) Yes?

PENGO We are getting on, Mr. Drury, both of us. We don't live forever.

DRURY Sometimes that thought is a comfort.

PENGO I have a Grand Design which will outwit mortality.

DRURY Don't tell me you are going into patent medicines!

PENGO The pictures. It concerns the ultimate destiny of the pictures.

DRURY What about them?

PENGO My idea is that you should endow a National Gallery of Art in this country—a counterpart of the National Gallery in London which you so admire. That your collection—when we have completed it—should be the first tenant of the Gallery, which indeed it would deserve to be.

DRURY Sounds like an expensive project.

PENGO Not too expensive for you, Mr. Drury. It will transform the hostility which surrounds you into gratitude. It will link your name eternally with the great artists. We pass. They go on. You will go on with them. (*He goes to the museum model—puts his hand on it*) Here is a model of the gallery made by the greatest of your architects.

DRURY (*With irony*) It is very generous of you, Lord Pengo, to give me the opportunity of endowing a gift of such magnitude.

PENGO You have done so much for your country already. It will be a monument forever. What panache! Princely tip to posterity. (*With a wave toward the throne*) He'd have done it. Lorenzo would have done it. In fact he did.

DRURY (*His voice rises*) Lorenzo was master of his destiny. He wasn't persecuted as I am! (PENGO *waits.* DRURY *gets control of himself, resumes in his normal voice*) The final irony. The government in Washington—the government for which I have done so much—is about to institute a tax suit against me, for over ten million dollars.

85

PENGO   That seems ungrateful.

DRURY   That man in the White House hates me. It is his personal revenge on me—for not supporting him. He has a genial smile, Mr. Roosevelt, but in his soul he is vindictive.

PENGO   (*Lightly, this is just what he wants; taps the model*) You know, Mr. Drury, the endowment I suggest might make this princely gift economical as well as generous. Circumvent oblivion and the collector of internal revenue at one stroke.

DRURY   (*After a moment, thinking hard*)   How?

PENGO   If you propose—and I shall be happy to testify in your tax suit that you have always proposed it—to give all your pictures to the nation, think what it will do for you, Mr. Drury. Your collection will be worth at least one hundred million dollars. How can even this administration have the effrontery to suggest that a man who has been striving to give away to the people a hundred million dollars has been simultaneously trying to rob them of ten? (*This makes a deep impression on* DRURY. *He sits, pondering, pondering. Gets up, walks to model again and looks at it with a new eye.* PENGO *presses his advantage*)   I do not mean to compare myself to you, Mr. Drury. No one is more aware—we are worlds apart. But one thing we do have in common—the climate. It is changing, Mr. Drury, and I have foreseen for a long time that it is changing.

DRURY   You are right. The climate *is* changing. Income and inheritance taxes—legalized confiscation. (*With bitter contempt*)   The welfare state! In a world where everything is going to belong to everybody, I shan't really care to live.

PENGO (*Comforts him*) There'll always be somebody to monopolize the welfare—corner the market in good will!

DRURY What a revolting idea! (*Stares at the throne*) That throne! An anachronism. This is no time for thrones!

PENGO (*Smoothly*) It will have a historic interest for those who visit your gallery. They will remember that you were the last emperor to have sat in it. (*A pause.* DRURY *sits staring, fascinated by the throne.* PENGO *keeps looking at* DRURY) When I first came to this country I observed what people like you were doing: in steel, in coal, in oil, in technology, in corporate finance. Mighty, unparalleled, imperial. To me it was a fantastic opera for which I was prepared to provide an expensive but imperishable setting. This opera—as you and your colleagues played it, Mr. Drury—is just about over. But you are lucky . . . (DRURY *looks up at him, sharply*) You own Titians and Raphaels, Botticellis and Giorgiones—they are linked with your name. You will find them valuable, Mr. Drury, as contemporary as well as eternal pals. (DRURY *says nothing. He sits, lost in a brown study*) You are lucky. You will have their companionship in heaven as you have it now on earth. Who will I have? (PENGO *decides it is a good moment to leave* DRURY *alone. He knows that what he has said has sunk in. As he goes, casually*) By the way—Scotus Slemp died without buying the Raphael Alba Madonna. She belongs in your collection, Mr. Drury. If you will excuse

me for a moment, I'll go down to arrange to have her
sent to you.

> (PENGO *goes out.* DRURY *sits. It has grown some-
> what dark in the room. Finally* DRURY, *still in a
> kind of trance, gets up. He looks at his watch. De-
> cides to go. His eye catches the throne again. He
> moves toward it, pauses. As if by a kind of automa-
> tism, he goes up to the steps that lead to the throne,
> gives a guilty look around to see that he is not being
> observed, and then sidles into the imperial seat*)

DRURY (*Safely seated, he muses out loud, involuntarily, as
if transported over the centuries by the grandeur and
antiquity of the chair*) Renaissance prince . . . misplaced . . . misplaced in time . . .

The lights dim

ACT TWO

SCENE 3

Scene: The same. Several hours later. It is snowing outside on this late fall afternoon. The lights are lit, soft radiance on the pictures from electroliers.

At rise: MISS SWANSON *is at her desk going over invoices.* VICKERS, *the accountant, comes in. He carries a cable in his hand. He is fit to be tied.*

VICKERS (*Shouts*)   I tell you, Miss Swanson, I can't stand it any more!

MISS SWANSON   I know how you feel. And yet you do. We all do.

VICKERS   Read this cable from London!
(*He gives* MISS SWANSON *the cable. She reads it, whistles faintly, but is calm. She returns it to* VICKERS)

MISS SWANSON   Well, as he left an unlimited order at Christie's, what do you expect?

VICKERS   He could have gone partners with Wellnew and got it for a third.

MISS SWANSON   Lord Pengo doesn't like to go partners.

VICKERS (*Taps the cable*)   Three hundred and seventy-five thousand for Pinkie!

MISS SWANSON Expensive child, Pinkie!

VICKERS Why, he sold it himself four years ago for a hundred. Who on earth does he think he can sell it to at this figure—to say nothing of a profit? I tell you, Miss Swanson, it's insane.

MISS SWANSON (*Wearily*) I have often suggested to Lord Pengo a motto for our front door: "Abandon sanity, all ye who enter here!"
  (PENGO *comes in. He is full of beans*)

PENGO Just been having tea with Mrs. Bovington. With Mrs. Bovington I have exactly the same relation that Disraeli had with Queen Victoria. And there is considerable resemblance.

MISS SWANSON Between you and Disraeli?

PENGO No, between Mrs. Bovington and Victoria. Mrs. B. is taller. But the same hats! (*Sees* VICKERS *stewing*) What's up, Vickers?

VICKERS (*With the heaviest sarcasm*) I congratulate you, Lord Pengo!

PENGO That's unusual. What about?

VICKERS (*Same voice*) On acquiring Lawrence's Pinkie!

PENGO (*Quickly*) Really! How much? (VICKERS *hands him the cable.* PENGO *takes it in at a glance*) Damn that Wellnew. A cabal . . . a conspiracy . . .

VICKERS Three hundred and seventy-five thousand dollars! For a picture everybody knows you sold yourself for a hundred. You'll never get rid of it—not at that figure. You'll never sell it at a profit—not possibly.

PENGO (*Quietly*) I don't want a profit.

VICKERS Are we in business for love?

PENGO (*Teasing him*) In a way . . .

VICKERS You'll have to sell it at a loss.

PENGO No matter what I sell it for—if I give it away—it won't be a loss.

VICKERS Is this a riddle?

PENGO Terwilliger wants this picture. He asked Wellnew to get it for him. I have to teach Terwilliger that if he wants a great picture *he can only get it from me!* They've got to learn that—all of them. They understand monopoly in *their* ventures—I understand it in mine!

MISS SWANSON (*Dryly*) Get it, Vickers?
    (*She goes out*)

VICKERS (*With passion*) Lord Pengo, you don't seem to realize I have to find three million dollars for the City Trust Bank tomorrow and I haven't got it. You promised me two million from Slemp. I won't mince words, my Lord—you face bankruptcy.

PENGO (*Quietly*) Get an extension.

VICKERS I've gotten one. I can't get another. It's a short-term note. It's up tomorrow.
    (PENGO *goes to his desk*)

PENGO (*At the phone*) Get Mr. McKenna, manager of the Drury Trust Company, Drury, Illinois. Mr. Vickers calling. (*He hangs up*) When Mr. McKenna calls, ask him for a three-million-dollar credit for sixty days. Mr. Drury has more than that amount of my stuff in his house right now. Tell him to call the City Trust to inform them that he is sending the draft. That will make the City Trust happy. I have two houses building in New York, Vickers; for Mrs. Drury and Mr. Brink. I shall ask Mr. Brink and Mrs. Drury to give me advances to cover the Drury draft within sixty days. That will make the Drury Trust happy. Will it make you happy?

VICKERS This job is getting to be a headache!

PENGO You lack faith, Vickers.
          (JOHNSON *comes in*)

JOHNSON Mrs. Enoch Drury.

PENGO Show her in, Johnson. (JOHNSON *goes*) There! You see, Vickers! The first of my two houses. Feel better?

VICKERS (*As he goes*) Except for my ulcer.
          (VICKERS *goes.* PRIMROSE *comes in. She has been crying and wears dark glasses to conceal it*)

PENGO My dear Primrose . . .

PRIMROSE (*Strained voice*) Hello, Joe. How's every little thing?

PENGO Why those glasses? Eye trouble?

PRIMROSE Don't want you to see my eyes, Joe . . . They're a sight . . .

PENGO Primrose, what is it? What's the matter?

PRIMROSE Come to say good-bye to you, Joe.

PENGO (*Astonished*) Good-bye?

PRIMROSE Yes, Joe.

PENGO Sir William Fitzpatrick was here with the plans for your house. He's got some marvelous plans, Prim. A colonnade . . . it'll be the only colonnade on Fifth Avenue.

PRIMROSE (*Flatly*) Not building the house, Joe.

PENGO This isn't like you, Prim! What's the matter?

PRIMROSE Just about everything. I'm sailin' to Europe tomorrow. For good. Not comin' back. Luckily, my analyst, Dr. Auerbach, is coming along. To keep me from jumpin' overboard, I guess.

PENGO (*Genuinely concerned*) What's happened? (*A silence*) Primrose, I'm your friend. House or no house —I'm your friend. You know that.

PRIMROSE That's why I came, Joe—to tell you. Derek doesn't know—you'll have to tell him.

PENGO I'm in the dark—

PRIMROSE So am I. In front of you, I guess, I can take these glasses off. (*She takes them off*) I'm still in the dark. (*Pitifully*) I feel as if—kinda— (*She laughs*) You always said I had a sunny nature, Joe.

PENGO And so you have. The sunniest I know.

PRIMROSE   Feel as if—I'll always be in the dark.

PENGO   Nonsense, I won't allow it! I love you, Prim. You
are very dear to me. Of all my clients—Derek knows it—
everyone knows it—you are the only one for whom I
feel—affection. Tell your friend Joe.

PRIMROSE   I know you meant well . . .

PENGO   I can't help you, darling, if you don't tell me what
it is!

PRIMROSE   (*Tries to be flippant*)   My romance, Joe, my
beautiful romance—well, Joe, I guess I was kidding myself! It's kind of on the rocks, Joe. Poor Derek. I tell you,
Joe, my heart breaks for Derek.

PENGO   (*In a terrible voice; an intimation of the disaster
begins to break on him*)   Oliver—you don't mean that
Oliver?

PRIMROSE   Yes, Joe. That's just what I mean. He liked me
for a time but I guess he kinda prefers Daphne.

PENGO   (*Stunned*)   Daphne—she's half his age!

PRIMROSE   I caught 'em, Joe—how do they call it—in—in—
I never can think of those funny foreign words you catch
people in.
        (*A silence*)

PENGO   I'll kill him. I'll break him.

PRIMROSE   (*Whose common sense never deserts her*)
What good'll that do? Will it put the pieces together for
me? (*A moment. He stares at her, fighting to control his
rage; if* OLIVER *were there at that moment he would*

94

break him in two) Say, Joe, something you *can* do for me. Tell Enoch he can have his divorce. Ain't gonner stand in his way any more. What for? It's selfish.

PENGO I'll kill him—I'll destroy that swine.

PRIMROSE *(Gravely—even with humor)* Daphne'd never forgive you for that. Heigh-ho. Easy come, easy go. Eh, Joe?

PENGO That nothing! That lightweight—when I think what I've done for him!

PRIMROSE Have you, Joe? What have you done for him? *(DEREK has come in, he overhears. He is very tense, eroded)*

DEREK Tell Primrose, Father, what you've done for Mr. Oliver!

PRIMROSE Hello, Derek.

DEREK Hello, Prim.

PRIMROSE *(Automatically)* Well, Derek, how's every little thing?

PENGO It seems absurd to me, dear Primrose, that on account of an elegant gutter-type like Oliver . . .

DEREK He's a gutter-type, is he?

PENGO *(Shouts)* What else?

DEREK How comes it, Father, with all your exalted connections, you have time also for gutter-types?

95

PRIMROSE (*Acutely; looks at Derek*) Guess you know the score, eh, Derek?

DEREK Yes, Prim. I know the score. Daphne just told me.

PRIMROSE Don't be hard on her, Derek.

DEREK Whether I am hard on her or not will make very little difference to Daphne!

PRIMROSE Poor kid! She never had a chance. My fault. Enoch's fault. Just look at the life she's had—the childhood she's had! Why, when she was six years old—right after Enoch left me, and I was takin' her abroad to get away from it all—Enoch's detectives kidnaped her right off the gangplank. So I didn't sail and *my* detectives kidnaped her right back. (*She laughs*) I remember Daphne's photograph all over the yellows. I have to laugh—just rememberin' one of the captions over her photograph. (*She traces with her fingers big letters*) *Bone of contention.* Poor Daphne, can you imagine— at the age of six—bein' a bone of contention? (*A moment; she appeals to Derek*) Don't be hard on Daphne, Derek. Maybe she'll get over it! (*Another moment of silence.* PENGO *realizes what a debacle this is—he is thinking hard*) Well, guess there's nothing much more to say. I'm sailin' tomorrow, Derek.

PENGO (*A last plea*) Wait! Why don't you wait? Give yourself time.

PRIMROSE Can't wait. My analyst's a very busy man. I had to talk him into taking his vacation now. He's got a bit of a crush on me, I think. Had to threaten suicide if he wouldn't.

PENGO Prim!

PRIMROSE Not that I ever *would* commit suicide. Something about doin' that that's in poor taste, I think. Leaves a bad impression. If I did that Daphne might blame herself and that wouldn't be fair to Daphne. (*As she passes* DEREK) 'Bye, Derek.

DEREK Good-bye, Prim. Bon voyage!

PRIMROSE (*A moment; she turns to* PENGO) Kiss me good-bye, Joe—just to show there's no hard feelin's about the house.
(PENGO *goes to her, kisses her. She turns and makes for the door swiftly. As she is on the verge of tears she whips her dark glasses on.* PRIMROSE *goes. The moment she is gone* PENGO *rushes to the phone*)

PENGO (*In a terrible voice*) I'll kill him!

DEREK (*Quietly*) I wouldn't do that, Father.

PENGO I'll kill him! I'll break him!

DEREK You can't do that.

PENGO Can't I?

DEREK You forget—he has Daphne. You engaged him to work on Primrose. Well, he worked on Daphne. She's now a prospective client. Almost as good, isn't it?

PENGO (*Wounded. He puts the receiver down, sits at desk —for a moment, defeated*) That's not fair, Derek.

DEREK Isn't it? Miss Swanson says that for you selling is a disembodied activity—like praying. Well, with Oliver

cozily married to Daphne, he can bring you votive offer-
ings, can't he? (*With bitterness*)   You can continue to
pray!

      (PENGO *gets up, faces* DEREK; *he is in a rage*)

PENGO   You sit in judgment on me! You are my son—for
whom I have planned everything—to whom I am going
to leave everything—and you sit in judgment on me!

DEREK   I begged you not to engage Oliver. I begged you.

PENGO   You're mooning over that spoiled little nympho-
maniac Daphne. I always felt she'd be no good for you.

DEREK   It's beyond that.

PENGO   Is it?

DEREK   Yes. It's beyond my destiny or hers or Prim's. It's
beyond that.

PENGO   Is it?

DEREK   It's the way you do business, your methods, mess-
ing up people's lives, throwing everything into the cash-
box—friendship, family, everything. Engaging gigolos to
woo them into building houses which you can furnish—
I want no part of it.

PENGO   (*Dangerously*)   Really?

DEREK   I am leaving, Father.

PENGO   Where for, may I ask?

DEREK   To Europe—possibly to Africa.

PENGO   To do what, may I ask?

DEREK   To paint.

PENGO   What makes you think you've got talent?

DEREK   I can only try.

PENGO   What about your mother?

DEREK   I've told her. She sympathizes. I go with her blessing.

PENGO   What sort of painting? These modern abstractionist daubs I suppose? Those Freudian nightmares in paint.

DEREK   We are not serene any more, Father. (*He points to the old masters on the wall*) We can't try to paint any more the way they did.

PENGO   I'm afraid not.

DEREK   We'll be better friends if we are separated.
         (*A silence.* PENGO *feels he has an advantage—he begins to woo* DEREK)

PENGO   In the first place you take these people—and their tribulations—much too seriously.

DEREK   I thought you were fond of Primrose . . .

PENGO   I adore her. How could you help it?

DEREK   Supposing she knew that Oliver is in your employ? That you engaged him to help you sell her the furnishing of a house?

PENGO   What's the harm in that?

DEREK   You see no harm in it? You see what it's done to her. To say nothing of what it's done to me!

99

PENGO   What's it done to her? These people are swayed by every emotional whim—they're rich enough to gratify every caprice. When something bothers them, there's always Europe, there's always their analysts. Don't you see, Derek—I try to give their amorphous lives some direction, some shape, some significance—through art—through beauty. If it weren't for me they wouldn't know what to do with themselves.

DEREK   Your gift for justifying yourself is really remarkable. It really is!

PENGO   It's the objective that counts, Derek. In my objective I am disinterested. Will it be remembered what I did and how I did it? What is important—if my plan comes through—is that *they* (*He gestures toward the paintings*) the pure, the innocent, the immortal—will find a home *there* (*He points to the model*) for generations yet unborn. Do you grudge me this dream? Do you grudge me my final absolution—this, yes, this wish to draw a mantle over myself to hide my sins? (*A moment; he adds dryly*) To say nothing of the sins of my clients.

DEREK   You're very plausible. That argument has been used before you. The end justifies the means.

PENGO   (*Quietly*) I think so. In this case, yes.

DEREK   It's always a special case.

PENGO   You forget, Derek, I haven't had the advantages of your education. I've had to make my way. I never studied abstract ethics at Oxford.

DEREK (*Aloud, as if to himself*) The ache Primrose feels —the ache I feel—the ache Mother feels—

PENGO (*Sharply; this reaches him*) Don't bring your mother into this! Your mother and I are all right! She loves me and I love her. There's no cloud between us— not a shadow . . .

DEREK No shadow. No cloud. I said ache.

PENGO (*Points to the model*) Once this is completed, I'll retire. Then your mother and I—you too if you like . . .

DEREK That perpetually receding some day—for how many years have we heard that?

PENGO You must be patient a little longer. I have been patient.

DEREK You have not been patient, Father. You have been —busy. You will go on being busy to the end. It'll go on to the end: your megaphoned buffooneries, butlers spying in houses, elegant scum like Oliver whispering inducements—all the dirty devices.

PENGO Be careful, Derek, be careful.

DEREK I'd better go.

PENGO (*Losing all control*) Go then. Good riddance. Go —go to Africa—go anywhere you like—paint your immature scrawls. See if you'll have any luck selling them!

DEREK Probably no luck.

PENGO I've given you everything—done everything for you.

101

DEREK   Yes, you have. Everything you could. And the result is . . .

PENGO   I see the result. That you despise me.

DEREK   Worse than that, Father. It is myself I despise.

PENGO   And with good reason!
(*There is a pause. They face each other, deadly enemies, and both devastated*)

DEREK (*Quietly*)   Exactly. With good reason. Good-bye, Father.

PENGO   Go then. Go and paint your silly pictures, but don't come whining back to me when you find—as you surely will find—that nobody wants them. Once you leave—you leave!

DEREK   That's my intention.

PENGO   Practice your lofty ethical standards in Africa. Elevate the natives! Get out! You depress me. Get out of my sight!

DEREK   I will. You'll be freer perhaps—with me out of the way.
(DEREK *goes.* PENGO *is seething with rage*)

PENGO (*Calls out*)   Derek. I didn't mean it . . . Derek, come back. (*No answer.* PENGO *gets up; he is in a kind of convulsion of rage and frustration. He finds himself in front of the Masaccio. All his rage is vented suddenly against the Masaccio. He shouts*)   Nobody wants it—nobody will buy it!
(*Obeying some dreadful compulsion he rips it off*

the wall and flings it across the room. MISS SWAN-
SON *comes in*)

MISS SWANSON (*Acutely distressed*)   What happened between you and Derek? He looked like a ghost. Wouldn't
speak to me. (*Sees the picture on the floor*)   I see that
the Masaccio has suffered an accident!

PENGO (*Fatalistically*)   Something is happening around
me. Something . . . a conspiracy . . . something . . .
(FILBERT *comes in*)

FILBERT   Wetmore just telephoned, my Lord. Mr. Drury
requests that you take back the Allendale.

PENGO (*Very quiet*)   Attend to that, Filbert.

FILBERT   Yes, my Lord.

PENGO (*To* MISS SWANSON)   I expected that. It's just as
well. I'll sell it to Terwilliger. (*To* FILBERT)   Get me
Walter Cannon Brink. Right away. (FILBERT *sits at the
desk, takes up the phone.* MISS SWANSON *keeps staring
at* PENGO. *She is full of compassion for him. To* MISS
SWANSON)   Primrose has given up the house. I wonder
how that will affect Brink?

FILBERT (*On the phone*)   Oh, Miss Williams—'ow do
you do, Miss Williams—Mr. Filbert speakin'—oh, you
'ave a message for Lord Pengo? (PENGO *walks up and
down, to get control, to think things out*)   Thank you,
Miss Williams. I will see that 'is Lordship gets the message.
(FILBERT *hangs up.* PENGO *faces him*)

PENGO   Well?

FILBERT   Mr. Brink 'as left the city. 'E 'as changed 'is mind about buildin' a 'ome in New York. 'E 'as instructed 'is lawyer to communicate with you, Lord Pengo.

(JOHNSON *comes in*)

JOHNSON   I am afraid I have bad news, your Lordship.

PENGO   Whenever you show your head it's bad news, Johnson. I am developing an acute prejudice against your head.

JOHNSON   I am sorry, your Lordship.

(*A moment*)

PENGO   Well?

JOHNSON   Word has just come. Phineas D. Terwilliger is dead.

PENGO   That's not possible.

JOHNSON   He was on his yacht—had an emergency operation for appendix—something went wrong—had he been on land . . .

PENGO   Two in one day. This begins to look like an epidemic! (*A silence.* PENGO *speaks not to them, aloud to himself*) Something secret, something sinister—I feel it —growing in the dark around me. Do you feel it, Johnson?

JOHNSON   In the midst of life we are in death.

PENGO   There is something pious about you, Johnson, that I have never liked.

JOHNSON   Yes, my Lord.

PENGO   That will be all. (*The two,* JOHNSON *and* FIL-
BERT, *start out, greatly relieved. As they go:*)   Don't
come in here unless you have something good to tell me.
That means probably that I'll never see either of you
again—which is a mitigating circumstance.

   (*After* FILBERT *and* JOHNSON *go out there is a long
   silence*)

MISS SWANSON   (*Finally; very moved—tender to him for
once*)   Quite a day, isn't it, Joe?

PENGO   Odd—like being ambushed in the dark—everything starts to crumble.

MISS SWANSON   (*Valedictory*)   You've had a good run, Joe.

PENGO   (*Gets up; this rouses him*)   If you think I'm
through, Miss Swanson, you're very much mistaken. I
have works of art that no one else in the world has.
They'll have to come to me for them—Drury, Brink, all of
them. I admit I was shaken for a minute, but that'll pass.
(*His voice rises*)   They'll have to come to me—and they
will—you hear—they will! (*A moment*)   Get me my
wife on the telephone.

   (MISS SWANSON *goes to desk, dials*)

MISS SWANSON   (*On the telephone*)   Lady Pengo? This is
Miss Swanson—Lord Pengo wants to speak to you.

   (*As* PENGO *goes to the phone,* MISS SWANSON *leaves
   the room*)

PENGO   (*On the telephone, most tender and affectionate*)
How are you, my dear? . . . Do I sound tired? . . .
That's odd because I feel wonderfully well—quite ex-

hilarated in fact . . . Did Derek tell you I simply can't make the Opera tonight? . . . I have a dreary evening ahead of me, but I must go through with it . . . I shall have my thoughts and they will be of you . . . No, my dearest one, no, you are wrong, because at the back of everything is the thought of that day when there'll just be you, whom I love very much indeed . . . and, darling . . . if you see Derek . . . I had a few words with him—afraid I lost my temper a bit. He's stubborn you know . . . but give him my love . . . not to you . . . you have it . . . Don't wait for me. I have a long dreary evening ahead of me. A new client . . . Sylvester Schmitt. He's taking me to the Holy Land. Pray for me. Good night, my love.

(*As he hangs up, the curtain falls*)

ACT THREE

ACT THREE

Scene: The same as Act Two; five years later. The pièce de résistance now is Rembrandt's Aristotle Contemplating the Bust of Homer, at the moment covered by a red velvet drapery. The Masaccio is still where it was, and Mrs. Siddons still hangs in the gallery.

At rise: MISS SWANSON *is at her desk. She is carefully putting selected papers into* LORD PENGO'S *open dispatch case.* PRIMROSE *comes in.* MISS SWANSON *rises to greet her.*

PRIMROSE   Hello, Miss Swanson! How's every little thing?

MISS SWANSON   Mrs. Auerbach! I've been expecting you.

PRIMROSE   When's Joe sailing?

MISS SWANSON   Tomorrow. You said on the telephone you had something to speak to me about.

PRIMROSE   Yes. I have. It's really my husband's idea . . . *(She hesitates)* Dr. Auerbach is a great man, you know. He certainly pulled me out of the slough of despond. I'd have been dead if not for him. *(Chuckles)* You know, Miss Swanson, his fees got to be so big I couldn't afford him any more. So I married him—as an economy.

MISS SWANSON   *(Dead pan)* Does he now give you a rate, Mrs. Auerbach?

PRIMROSE   Minute I married him, I didn't need him—

professionally. (*A moment.* MISS SWANSON *is waiting*)
It's a bit touchy—what I want to speak to you about.

MISS SWANSON   You need have no hesitation. I am here to
serve Lord Pengo's friends.

PRIMROSE   It's about Daphne. We got a problem with
Daphne. Ever since that awful scandal with Mr. Oliver
. . . Daphne's been so . . . they call it disturbed . . .
that it's got Jerome and me worried.

MISS SWANSON   I'm sorry.

PRIMROSE   The thing is this. You know Daphne and
Derek have been corresponding . . .

MISS SWANSON   Yes, Mrs. Auerbach?

PRIMROSE (*Comes to* MISS SWANSON *anxiously*)   If you
sent for Derek. If Joe did. If you got Derek back here.
Some trumped-up excuse. So it'd seem casual. So they
might begin seeing each other again. Do you think I
could speak to Joe about it? (*A silence.* PRIMROSE *mis-
understands her silence*)   Do you think I'm just plain
nuts, Miss Swanson? (*Her voice rises*)   I'm just about
fit to be tied about Daphne . . .

MISS SWANSON (*Finally, her voice is quiet but tense*)   I
don't have to send for Derek, Mrs. Auerbach. I have already sent for him. Derek is here.

PRIMROSE (*Amazed*)   You don't say!

MISS SWANSON   Derek arrived this morning. I'm expecting him now.

PRIMROSE (*Looks at her shrewdly*)   Why did you send
for him?

MISS SWANSON   For reasons of my own, Mrs. Auerbach!

PRIMROSE   Does Joe know Derek is here?

MISS SWANSON   Not yet. I wanted to surprise Lord Pengo.

PRIMROSE   (*Affected*)   My God, Miss Swanson! Is it as bad as that? I know Joe hasn't been feeling too good—but is it as bad as that?

MISS SWANSON   I said, Mrs. Auerbach, for reasons of my own!

PRIMROSE   (*Sadly*)   Aw, come on, Miss Swanson, I'm not as dumb as I look. Is Joe as sick as all that? Is there to be no more Joe?

MISS SWANSON   Lord Pengo is very strong, Mrs. Auerbach. He's tired. He just needs a little rest.

PRIMROSE   (*Knows* MISS SWANSON *is lying*)   If anything happened to Joe . . . I don't know . . . life wouldn't be the same . . . something'd have gone out of it . . . that you couldn't get back . . . for me anyway.
(*A moment's silence.* DEREK *walks in. He is older but looks sunburned and well. The London elegance has gone. He is now carelessly dressed, his tie askew. He feels emotion at seeing* MISS SWANSON—*doesn't notice* PRIMROSE *for a moment*)

MISS SWANSON   Derek!

DEREK   Miss Swanson! (*He puts his arms around her, kisses her on the cheek—sees* PRIMROSE, *goes to her*) Prim! How marvelous! Prim!

PRIMROSE   (*Embraces and kisses him*)   Derek! (*She holds him off, looks at him)* You look marvelous! You look like a million dollars!

DEREK *(Laughs)* How could I get in here if I didn't! *(He looks around the room)* Five years! And everything exactly the same! Miss Swanson at Father's desk. How's Daphne?

PRIMROSE She's kinda . . . she'll be awful glad to see you, Derek.

DEREK I'll be happy to see her.

PRIMROSE Maybe we can arrange something for tonight.

DEREK That would be fine.

PRIMROSE Well, I know you'll be wanting to talk to Miss Swanson. I'll just go up and have a look around . . . *(As she goes to the door)* Oh, Miss Swanson. Next week is our anniversary—Jerome's and mine. I'd like to pick up something for him.

MISS SWANSON Shall I ring for Johnson?

PRIMROSE Do you think I need Johnson? I know this place better than Johnson. I'll look around till Joe comes. I want it to be something kinda special. Let me know the minute Joe comes, will you? (MISS SWANSON *nods)* So good to have you back, Derek. Daphne'll be delighted!

DEREK Give her my love.

PRIMROSE I sure will! *(With a little chuckle)* She's just about ready for it!

      (PRIMROSE goes out. MISS SWANSON and DEREK are alone. MISS SWANSON lifts her head from the

memoranda. DEREK *walks around the room. He un-veils the Rembrandt)*

DEREK What a marvelous Rembrandt! Dad certainly gets them, doesn't he?

MISS SWANSON Yes. He gets them.

DEREK How is he, Miss Swanson?

MISS SWANSON That's why I sent for you, Derek.

DEREK You said it was because he wanted to see me but was too proud to ask me to come.

MISS SWANSON You know how terribly you felt—when your mother died so suddenly—and you weren't here.

DEREK (*After a moment*) Is it like that?

MISS SWANSON I think this will be his last trip to Europe. I want you to sail with him. I want you to be with him. (*A moment*) Don't say I had anything to do with it.

DEREK Of course not. Bless you for sending for me. Does he know?

MISS SWANSON Of course he does. He's known for the last four years. But never a word out of him.

DEREK Has it slowed him up?

MISS SWANSON Not in the least. He's going stronger than ever. Right this minute he's pulling off the biggest project of his career. The Terwilliger Collection. He's as excited as if it were his first deal.

DEREK You said once that with him selling was a disembodied activity—like praying.

MISS SWANSON   Yes. Like the saints, he will die praying!

DEREK (*At the model, his hand on it*)   After he finished this—his Grand Design—he was going to begin to live. Well, this is now a reality. He's a great man, Miss Swanson.

MISS SWANSON   Of course he is. They ought to put up a statue to him.

DEREK   Does he ever refer to our quarrel?

MISS SWANSON   No. But it shook him. I know he hasn't forgotten it.

DEREK   I was insufferable.

MISS SWANSON   You had your point.

DEREK   I suppose so. But actually . . . you know . . .

MISS SWANSON   Well?

DEREK   It sounded like righteous indignation . . . but the truth is . . . it was jealousy . . . jealousy of Oliver . . . frustration over Daphne.
     (MISS SWANSON, *in neatening up the desk, has picked up the photograph of Lady Pengo*)

DEREK (*Takes the photograph from her and looks at it*) Wherever he was—in hotel rooms and houses everywhere —the first thing Father always did was to unpack this picture of Mother.

MISS SWANSON   Yours too.

DEREK   And now she's gone. How she waited and waited for that "some day" that Father was always promising her. It never came.

MISS SWANSON Some day. Does it ever come? For anybody? . . . I suppose mine will come when I retire to
my mother's cottage in Glens Falls. And do you know
what I'll be doing there? Thinking back on all that went
on here in this room—all the dealing and sharpshooting
—and how wonderful and exciting it was, during all
those thirty-five years, just to be *near* your father. (MISS
SWANSON *derives comfort somehow from the fact that*
DEREK *now shares her secret. The intercom buzzes*)
Yes? (*She hangs up; to* DEREK) It's your father. He's
on the way up. (*She starts for her office*) Remember—
you haven't a notion . . . And, Derek, tell him how well
he's looking!

DEREK (*Very moved*) Trust me.
            (MISS SWANSON *exits.* DEREK *hears steps approach-
            ing and goes quickly to the Rembrandt, pretending
            to lose himself in it.* PENGO *enters. He looks older.
            He is still vibrant and vital, but, somehow, his
            clothes hang a bit loosely on him and you get the
            feeling, in some indefinable way, that he is mortally
            stricken*)

PENGO (*Sees* DEREK—*unable to believe his eyes*) Derek!
Derek!

DEREK Father! It's good to see you!

PENGO If I hadn't become an Englishman—and a member
of the House of Lords . . . I should give way to my
feelings. (*They stand looking at each other*) After all
—I'm Hungarian—why not? (*He embraces* DEREK,
quickly, impulsively, awkwardly—grins)

DEREK You're looking wonderful!

PENGO (*Cheerfully*) It's apoplexy! But you, Derek, you . . . (*He surveys him*) Painting in *plein air* agrees with you. You look wonderfully healthy. (*Surveying his costume critically*) Can't say I like your tie.

DEREK I'll borrow one of yours.

PENGO (*Severely*) Nor is it tied properly. In fact it isn't tied at all . . . do you mind if I . . . I am reconciled to your *being* an artist, but I don't want you to look like one!
(*He straightens* DEREK's *tie*)

DEREK I'm afraid I don't suit the premises.

PENGO Suit them! You clash with them. But I see you noticed that Rembrandt.

DEREK It would be hard not to notice it.

PENGO How do you like it?

DEREK (*As they stand before the Rembrandt*) It's glorious!

PENGO (*Teasing him a bit*) They weren't bad in their way, were they—the old fellows?

DEREK (*Takes his father's tone*) No—in their way they weren't bad!

PENGO Aristotle. I can't say I've read him, but now that I own him I feel very close to him. Greatest Rembrandt I ever owned. Greatest Rembrandt anybody ever owned.

DEREK (*Laughs*) You forget, Dad—I'm not a customer! But I'm delighted to find you in such good spirits.

PENGO Why shouldn't I be? Everything's going marvelously. Just left Drury. He's dying. (*Quickly, obviating a possible misunderstanding*) I don't mean that's why I'm in good spirits. We're great pals now, Drury and I. What do you think I found him doing? He was sitting on that Renaissance throne I sold him—remember that throne, Derek?

DEREK (*A humorous rapport between them*) I remember it very well. As good a throne as you'd find anywhere.

PENGO (*With a hint of reprimand*) You wouldn't find a throne like that anywhere. You'd just find it here. Well, there he was, poor Drury, sitting on that throne. The organ he's had installed in the house I built for him was playing "Silver Threads Among the Gold." He was chewing gum and reading *The Saturday Evening Post.* (DEREK *laughs*) He showed me with great pride a letter he'd received from the President of the United States, thanking him for donating that (*Points to model*) to the American people. If there's any one man in the world Drury hates it's F.D.R., and yet he's as pleased as a little boy over that letter. There's something about the Presidency that impresses people. (*He chuckles at his own conceit, and as he feels response from* DEREK, *he gets more and more wound up. He puts his hand on* DEREK's *shoulder*) It's a funny thing, Derek—there are only two of my giants left—Drury and Sylvester Schmitt. You remember Sylvester Schmitt?

DEREK The Burton Holmes man?

PENGO That's right. He's dying, too. I'm the special emissary between the two deathbeds. I give them daily bulletins about each other. Schmitt will say: "How was Drury when you saw him yesterday?" I say, "Terrible."

That gives Schmitt a nip-up. Drury will say: "How's that vulgarian Schmitt?" "Awful," I say. That bucks Drury up. The funny thing is, Derek . . .

DEREK Yes?

PENGO The funny thing is—here are these two men—both dying—and all that remains to them is the art I sold them. You take Schmitt—I was with him the morning he had to say good-bye to his pictures, before sending them (*He points to model*) over there. It was like a father losing his children. I did my best to console him—I said that his children were going to a good home and would be well cared for. Still—when they were taken away—he wept. I'm ashamed to say, I did too . . . In the chill that surrounds them, in the fear they feel, their only comfort, their only warmth, is the glow that comes to them from my pictures. Their families have disappointed them, their money and their power no longer sustain them, they are generally hated, but the pictures are their loyal friends and companions—the pictures are their accomplishment and their pride. They forget that I supplied them and— (*He grins at* DEREK) I am too tactful to remind them.

DEREK There's no one like you, Father. There never was.

PENGO (*Reminiscently*) It has been amusing. I've enjoyed it.

DEREK And what makes me happy is that you're still enjoying it.

PENGO (*A pause. He looks at his son with deep tenderness*) I can't tell you, Derek, how pleased I am to see you.

118

DEREK I can't tell you, Father, how happy I am to see you.

PENGO (*Briskly, to get away from emotion*) What are you doing in New York?

DEREK I hesitate to tell you.

PENGO Don't hesitate. My clients do that. It makes me nervous. Don't you do it!

DEREK Well, Father, the fact is . . . the simple fact is . . .

PENGO Well?

DEREK I missed you and wanted to see you.

PENGO (*Quietly*) I am very touched, my boy.

DEREK Also . . .

PENGO Yes?

DEREK I have come to feel that in the issue between us—that terrible quarrel we had—that I was wrong. I've worked at my painting. I haven't spared myself. But I've come to realize . . . I'm not a great talent. I'll never set the Thames on fire, I'm just clever. Not good enough. I would like, if you will have me, to come back into the business.

PENGO I won't take you!

DEREK You're still angry then?

PENGO My dear boy . . . you quite misunderstand. I won't take you because—in the issue between us—in the quarrel we had—you were right. It was I who was wrong. You stick to what you're doing. I am gross, you are sensitive. I am predatory, you are an idealist. I am a huckster, you have a dream of creation. In short, you are an artist. Having sold dead artists all my life, I cannot tell you how proud I am, my boy, to have a live artist in the family. No. No. You go back to France and paint. I'll be in England for a bit and we can see each other.

DEREK (*Playing it out*) Well, it's a graceful rejection.

PENGO Rejection?

DEREK Well, isn't it? Nicely put, of course.

PENGO I am not going to allow a momentary discouragement to push you off course. We're different temperaments. Totally different. I'm an exhibitionist. I've put on a performance. I've enjoyed it. But occasionally I ask myself: "What are you, beneath the performance?"

DEREK And what is your reply to that question?

PENGO I always refuse to answer—on advice of counsel.

DEREK I will not allow you to underrate yourself. I see now what I didn't see when I was younger and knew it all—that you are—do you know what you really are?—a visionary. Except that, unlike most visionaries, you have the gift of reality.

PENGO (*With a darting smile at him*) Well, I am aware there is plenty of ground for criticism, but do you know, when I look back—when I think of my opportunities—I am dazzled by my moderation. But didn't somebody say that ahead of me?

DEREK They did, but you might have invented it. (*A moment*) Miss Swanson tells me you're sailing tomorrow.

PENGO That's right.

DEREK Since you won't take me back in the business, I've got nothing to do here. Couldn't I sail with you?

PENGO Would you? Would you really?

DEREK I'd love to. I'm rather at loose ends, as a matter of fact.

PENGO (*Overjoyed*) Well, I'll tighten them up. Are you free for dinner?

DEREK Free as a bird.

PENGO Good. I'll get Prim and Daphne.

DEREK Fine.

PENGO Speaking of Daphne . . . (*Suddenly struck by a marvelous idea*) My God, Derek, Daphne! (*He takes his arm and starts walking him across the room, his voice dropping to a confidential whisper*) You know all about Daphne. The marriage to Oliver was a disaster. I'm responsible for that, in a way. I feel considerable guilt over that. Now, Derek, I can make handsome amends to Daphne!

DEREK How?

PENGO Daphne's crazy about you. She's never forgotten you. She realizes what a mistake she made. You and Daphne! What you always wanted. Don't sail with me. Stay and woo Daphne. No, I've got a better idea. I'll get Daphne to sail with us . . .

(*He lunges to the telephone to make a reservation*)

DEREK Don't do that, Father.

PENGO Why not?

DEREK Because it's impossible—there's something I have to tell you—I was going to tell you on the boat but I'd better tell you now.

PENGO What?

DEREK I'm engaged to be married.

PENGO To whom?

DEREK My model.

PENGO Model!

DEREK Just before I sailed I asked her to marry me.

PENGO (*With mounting anger*) You mean to say you're going to marry a French peasant girl when Daphne . . .

DEREK (*Quiet but firm*) Yes, Father, that is what I am going to do.

PENGO (*In a towering rage*) It's insane! It's idiotic . . . it's . . .

DEREK Please, Father, don't work yourself up!

PENGO But it's so stupid! You're throwing your life away!

DEREK I don't think so.

PENGO Really, it's too—Bohemian! You've just said you don't believe in your talent. Do you think you'll increase it by marrying a model? Are you imitating the great artists who married their models? I should think you'd try to become a great artist first.

DEREK Please, Father, don't let's quarrel again.

PENGO (*The enormity of it grows on him*) Here's Daphne—crazy about you—waiting for you—the girl you always wanted!

DEREK I no longer want her. Father, I want you to meet Yvette.

PENGO I have no wish to meet Yvette. (*Repeats contemptuously the commonplace name*) Yvette!

DEREK She's a dear girl and I'm happy with her, Father.

PENGO But you were in love with Daphne for so long . . . You wanted no one in the world but Daphne!

DEREK I suffered over Daphne. Daphne cannot make me suffer again.

PENGO Is that why you won't marry her—because she can no longer make you suffer?

DEREK Do you want me to marry Daphne just to absolve your sense of guilt over Oliver?
(*The question is searching. It stops* PENGO)

PENGO (*After a pause*) Perhaps you're right, Derek. I see what you mean. I'm sorry. I apologize. (*He snaps out of it*) What fun it will be—sailing with you. Now, Derek, tell you what—where are you staying?

DEREK The Penfield.

PENGO Never heard of it. Can't be any good. You shall move to the St. Regis where I have more room than I can use.

DEREK Delighted.

PENGO As it's my last afternoon here I have a few things

to clean up. Get out of your hotel and meet me at the St. Regis in an hour.

DEREK   Right.

PENGO   Do you mind if I ask Daphne for dinner?

DEREK   Not at all. I'd love to see her.
   (FILBERT *comes in*)

FILBERT   Good to 'ave Mr. Derek back, your Lordship!

PENGO   Very good. You know, Filbert, he's sailing with me.

FILBERT   Indeed! Wonderful.

PENGO   Now then, Filbert, about this Texan, Slocum . . . (*To* DEREK) Since you left, Derek, I've invaded Texas!

DEREK   Was Texas responsive?

PENGO   My dear boy, where art is concerned, Texas is a virgin—a colossal and immensely rich and eager virgin —waiting to be ravished.

DEREK   Hope you won't hold her up too long!

PENGO   Oh, she's got to learn that in the field of art there is, between passion and consummation, an anxious interval!

FILBERT   Mr. Slocum 'as written askin' for an immediate appointment.

PENGO   (*As of yore, puts on a show for* DEREK) Well, he can't have it, as I am sailing. But you see him and sell him Mrs. Siddons. He's ripe—I've conditioned him. (*He looks at Mrs. Siddons*) She's almost too good for Texas.

Still, stretch a point. That's about all, Filbert. See you at the boat. Ask Miss Swanson to come in. And Mrs. Auerbach.

FILBERT Mrs. Auerbach is looking for something for 'er 'usband, your Lordship. She turns up 'er nose at everything I show 'er.

PENGO Does she?

FILBERT Yes, my Lord.

PENGO For her husband, you say?

FILBERT Yes, my Lord. For their third wedding anniversary. It's got to be something special, she says.

PENGO Special . . . (*His face lights up—he's got it*) Send her in here, Filbert. I'll give her something special.

FILBERT Yes, your Lordship.
        (FILBERT *goes*)

PENGO Admirable fellow, Filbert. No brains. Have to leave everything to Miss Swanson, who has plenty. Yet I shall miss him tomorrow on the *Berengaria*.

DEREK Well, Dad, you can't have everything!

PENGO (*Mock defiance*) Who says you can't!
        (PRIMROSE *comes back*)

PRIMROSE There's nothing any good in your shop any more, Joe.

DEREK I'll see you at dinner, Prim.

PRIMROSE Lovely. I spoke to Daphne. She's joining us.

DEREK Couldn't be nicer.

PRIMROSE (*With a fond look*) Daphne'll be so pleased! (DEREK *goes. She looks after* DEREK *fondly*) Gosh, that's a nice boy. What a stupid girl Daphne is—she could have saved herself all that trouble.

PENGO Daphne may be stupid but Derek isn't very bright either, I regret to say.

PRIMROSE Why?

PENGO He's going to marry an anonymous French girl.

PRIMROSE (*This is a blow to her*) Really?

PENGO (*Depressed by it too*) I'm afraid so.

PRIMROSE Damn!

PENGO Same here! Double damn. (*Broods for a moment*) As I say—I love Derek, but he's not very bright.

PRIMROSE (*A pause*) Well, there's nothing to do, is there?

PENGO Nothing at all.

PRIMROSE (*Snaps out of it*) Say, Joe, I'm desperate for something to give Jerome for our third anniversary.

PENGO I've got just the thing—a marvelous thing—that will make him happy forever.

PRIMROSE I'd love to give him something that will make him happy forever—in case I can't!

PENGO Come here, Prim.
(*With solemnity, as becomes the presence of a masterpiece,* PENGO *walks impressively upstage.* PRIMROSE *follows him, dutifully.* PENGO *pauses in front of the Masaccio. Points to it dramatically*) This

picture—which Bernard Berenson has called one of the masterpieces of Renaissance painting—The Circumcision, by Masaccio.

PRIMROSE (*Peers at it*) Ain't it kinda dark? Ain't it kinda gloomy?

PENGO To you, perhaps. It won't be to your husband. Remember he is a doctor. It will have a professional interest for him—as well as racial.

PRIMROSE (*Impressed*) Gee, sounds just right for him, don't it?

PENGO I believe that Masaccio painted it—four centuries ago—with Jerome in mind.

PRIMROSE I suppose you'll want a packet for it.

PENGO Oh, more than that, Prim! Your husband is an eminent man. The possession of this picture will make him unique.

PRIMROSE Okay, Joe. Wrap it up.
    (MISS SWANSON *returns*)

MISS SWANSON Derek's fixed up for tomorrow. "A" deck. Not far from you.

PENGO Good! (*He walks* PRIMROSE *to the door*) See you soon, Prim.

PRIMROSE What time?

PENGO Eight-thirty!

PRIMROSE Fine. (*Pauses at the door*) Shall I tell the bad news to Daphne?

PENGO   No, no. Why mention it? Maybe she can break it up. She's done it before.

PRIMROSE   You cheer me up, Joe. You really do.
(PRIMROSE *goes. The moment she has gone,* PENGO *gives way to ecstasy. He is so jubilant that he runs to* MISS SWANSON *who is bending over the desk putting memoranda into* PENGO's *dispatch case, and slaps her on the rear. The papers drop from* MISS SWANSON's *hands*)

MISS SWANSON   Lord Pengo!

PENGO   What do you think, Miss Swanson? What do you think?

MISS SWANSON   Well, I must say, Lord Pengo, I don't know what to think!

PENGO (*Crows in triumph*)   I've sold it. I've sold that damn Masaccio!

MISS SWANSON   Is that all?

PENGO   Is that all! You say is that all. Do you know how long that bloody picture has been hanging on my walls, here and in London? For thirty-five years. No one would buy it. No one. I couldn't give it away. And now I just sold it to Prim. Can you imagine a better present for a psychiatrist? Why, it's like selling it to Sigmund Freud himself. (*During this hymn* MISS SWANSON, *back at her desk, never lifts her head from her papers*)   Well, Miss Swanson, it's been a good day!

MISS SWANSON   I'm glad you call it a good day!

PENGO   Well, isn't it? Derek's return and I got rid of the

Masaccio. (*Suddenly suspicious*) By the way—Derek
—you had nothing to do with that, had you?

MISS SWANSON   Nothing whatever. Derek never let me
know he was coming. I was as surprised as you were.

PENGO (*Very brisk and business-like*) One last thing,
Miss Swanson, about the Terwilliger Collection. I'm
negotiating about it with Drury. He says I ask too much.

MISS SWANSON   And so you do.

PENGO   I always have. Why should I change now? My
idea is this: to repeat my technique with the Lane Collection. The sculpture and tapestries in the collection
Drury isn't interested in—just the paintings. If he will
pay fifteen million for them, I will offer that for the
collection. Then I will give Drury the paintings, so that
I shall get the sculpture and the tapestries for nothing.

MISS SWANSON   I guess they're worth that!

PENGO   In other circumstances I would fire you for that
remark, Miss Swanson.

MISS SWANSON   In other circumstances I should welcome
it!
       (*He gives her a sharp look*)

PENGO   Well, Miss Swanson, I think you might be a bit
more gracious, considering I am leaving tomorrow and
won't be back for a considerable time.

MISS SWANSON   Sorry. I'll try.

PENGO   You know, Miss Swanson, no matter what you
may think, I never felt better in my life. I know that
Dr. Gumbach takes a poor view of me and that you

have talked to Dr. Gumbach. But let me remind you that I've outlived four doctors. I confidently expect to outlive Dr. Gumbach.

MISS SWANSON (*Bent over her papers*) I am sure you will.

PENGO (*After a moment*) Well, Miss Swanson, I guess that's all. (*A pause.* PENGO *looks around the room. He knows that he will never see it again. He walks to the Rembrandt, stares at it*) I hate to see the last of this beautiful Rembrandt. (*As one pronouncing an odd doom mournfully*) He'll end up in Texas!

MISS SWANSON You can go to Texas to see him.

PENGO (*Musing aloud in front of the Rembrandt*) I didn't feel well in Texas. Don't think I'll ever make that trip again. I do confess, Miss Swanson, I feel a bit tired. I think, after I've settled some immediate business in London, I'll go to the country and rest for a while. I have this lovely place in Kent and yet I've never spent more than a weekend there.

MISS SWANSON That's an excellent idea—but you won't do it! (MISS SWANSON *pours water from a carafe into a glass and takes a pill from a little silver box*) Take your pill.

PENGO I think today I'd better have two. (MISS SWANSON *hesitates, then takes out another pill and gives it to him*) Well, Miss Swanson, I guess that's all. See you at the boat! (*At this* MISS SWANSON's *iron control deserts her without warning. She starts sobbing into her handkerchief.* PENGO *is startled and concerned*) Why, Miss Swanson, what's the matter? (MISS SWANSON *shakes her head without lifting it*) I *will* see you at the boat,

won't I? (MISS SWANSON *nods without lifting her head.*
PENGO *comes close to her; in an altered voice*) Well,
there's no use pretending with you, is there? There
never has been. Anyway, we've had an interesting time,
haven't we? Outside of you, I've fooled everybody for
four years. That's pretty good. Isn't it? (*A moment.*
MISS SWANSON'S *face is still invisible.* PENGO *doesn't
know what to do, quite*) I am flattered, Miss Swanson.
It proves that I could not have been such a bad boss
after all. Really—by the way, Miss Swanson—my God,
I can't believe it! I really can't believe it. I had an impulse just now to call you by your first name and it
suddenly struck me—I don't *know* your first name. Isn't
it awful? Please, Miss Swanson, tell me your first name.

MISS SWANSON (*Muffled, from her handkerchief*) Edna.

PENGO Thank you. Dear Edna. Dearest Edna, thank you
for everything. (*A moment. It is important for* PENGO
to keep MISS SWANSON *from getting too emotional and
he knows how to do it*) And one more thing, there's
something else I've forgotten. Miss Swanson—Edna—
get Severance on the phone and tell him to meet me
at the boat tomorrow. It's important!

MISS SWANSON (*Lifts her head and rasps at him*) What
do you want with that old fuss-budget? Haven't you
gassed with him enough?

PENGO (*With dignity*) You forget he is my lawyer.

MISS SWANSON What are you selling *him?*

PENGO You misunderstand me. You underrate me. In my
will I've left you a percentage of the business. Now that

131

I know that you feel for me so deeply, I certainly intend
to increase your percentage!

> (*That does it! Furious,* MISS SWANSON *makes an
> angry gesture and runs out of the room. Left alone,*
> PENGO *picks up the glass and swallows the second
> pill. He gets up, and looks around the room. He
> walks to the Rembrandt; he makes a tour of the
> room, pauses before Mrs. Siddons. He goes to the
> model, touches it, goes to the desk, puts his wife's
> photograph into the open dispatch case, snaps it
> shut. Carrying it, he starts to go. As he turns, the
> Masaccio catches his eye. In affectionate farewell,
> he waves to the Masaccio and goes out through the
> sky-lighted gallery)*

Curtain

E